COME WALK WITH ME

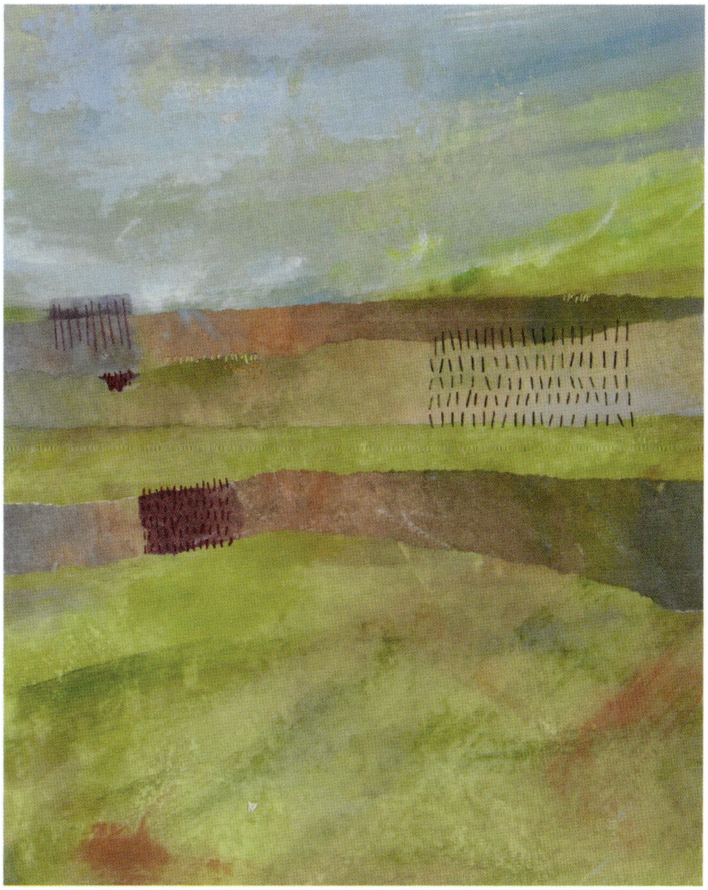

Wine Fields
Washi paper collage and stitch, 14" × 18" (36cm ×58cm)

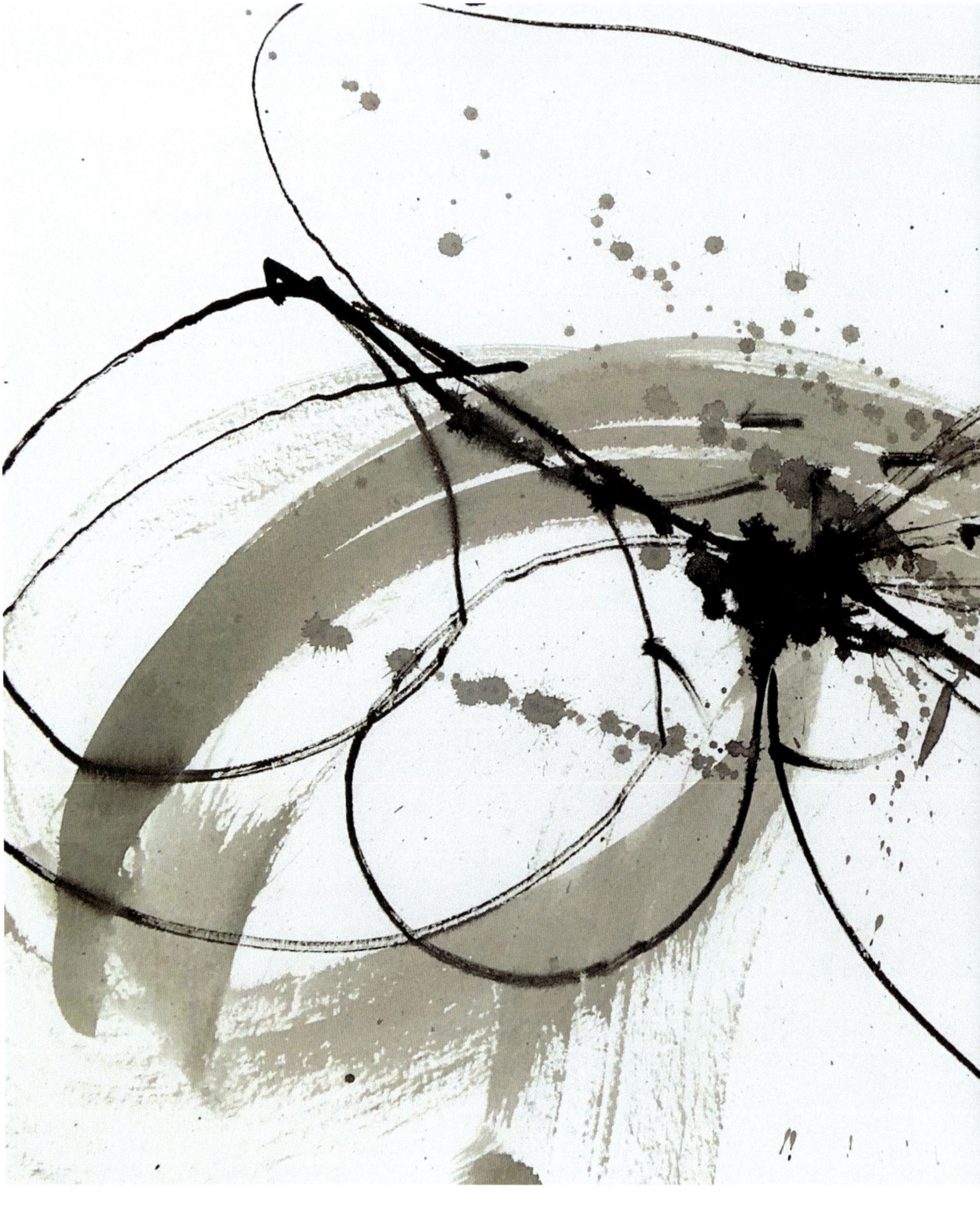

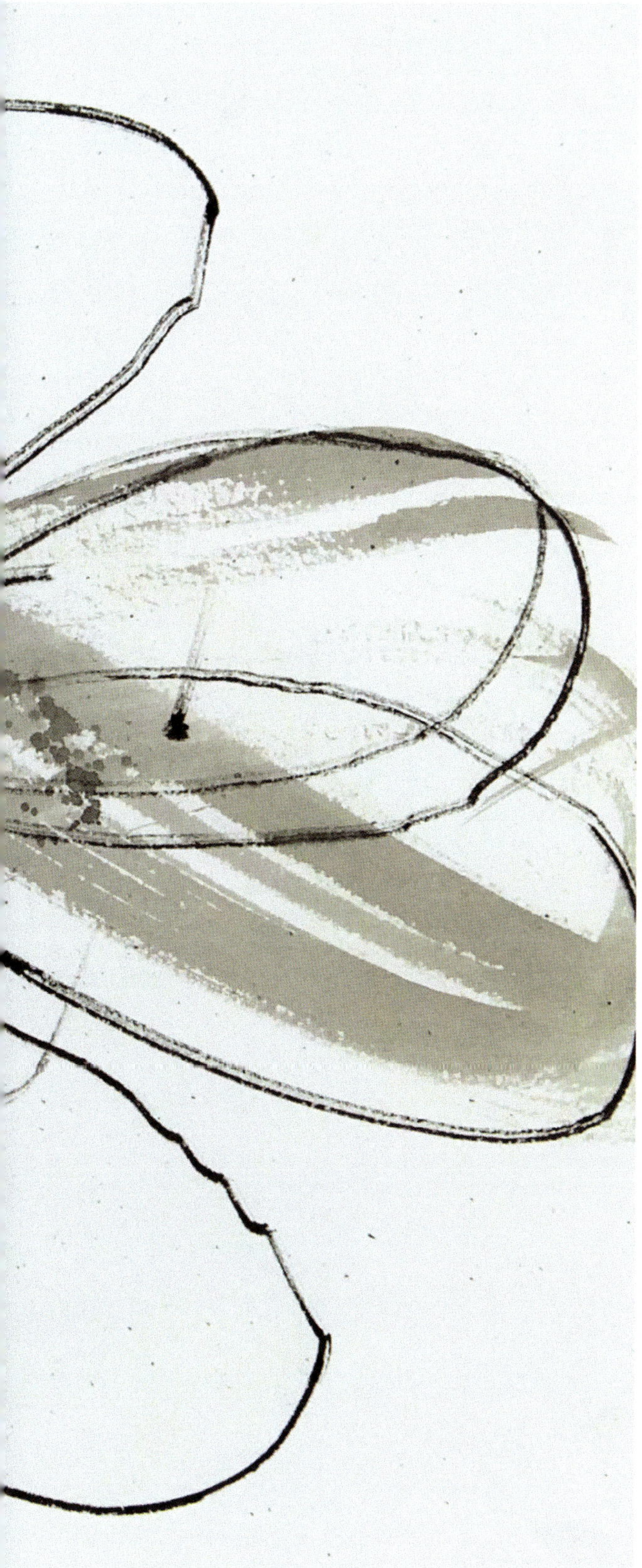

COME WALK WITH ME

EXPLORING WHY ART MATTERS

ROBERTA WAGNER

For Bruce Bugbee with all my love

With a special thank you to his good friend, John Kirry, for help with the photographs

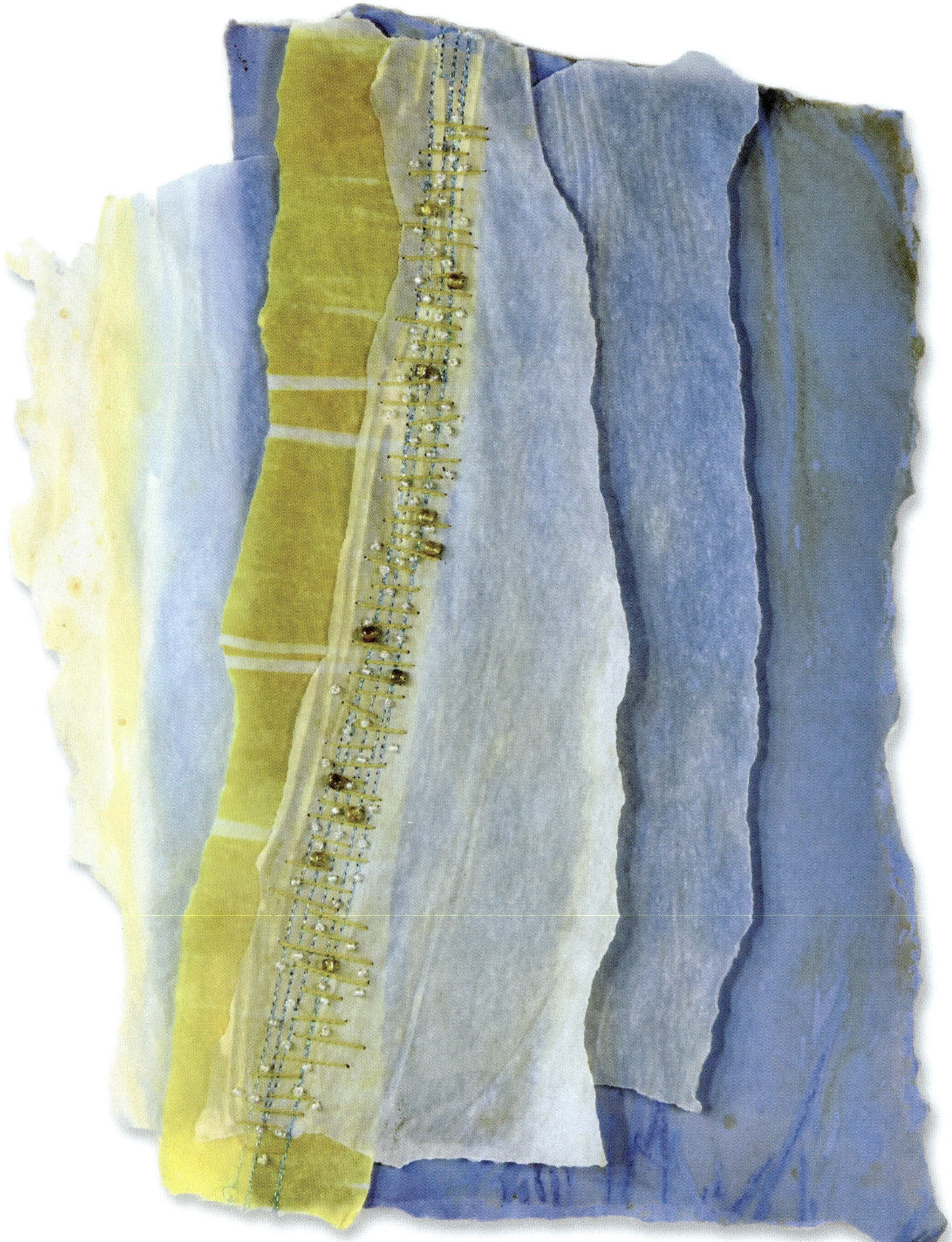

Tidelands
Botanically-dyed papers, stitch and beads; 8" × 11" (20cm × 28cm)

CONTENTS

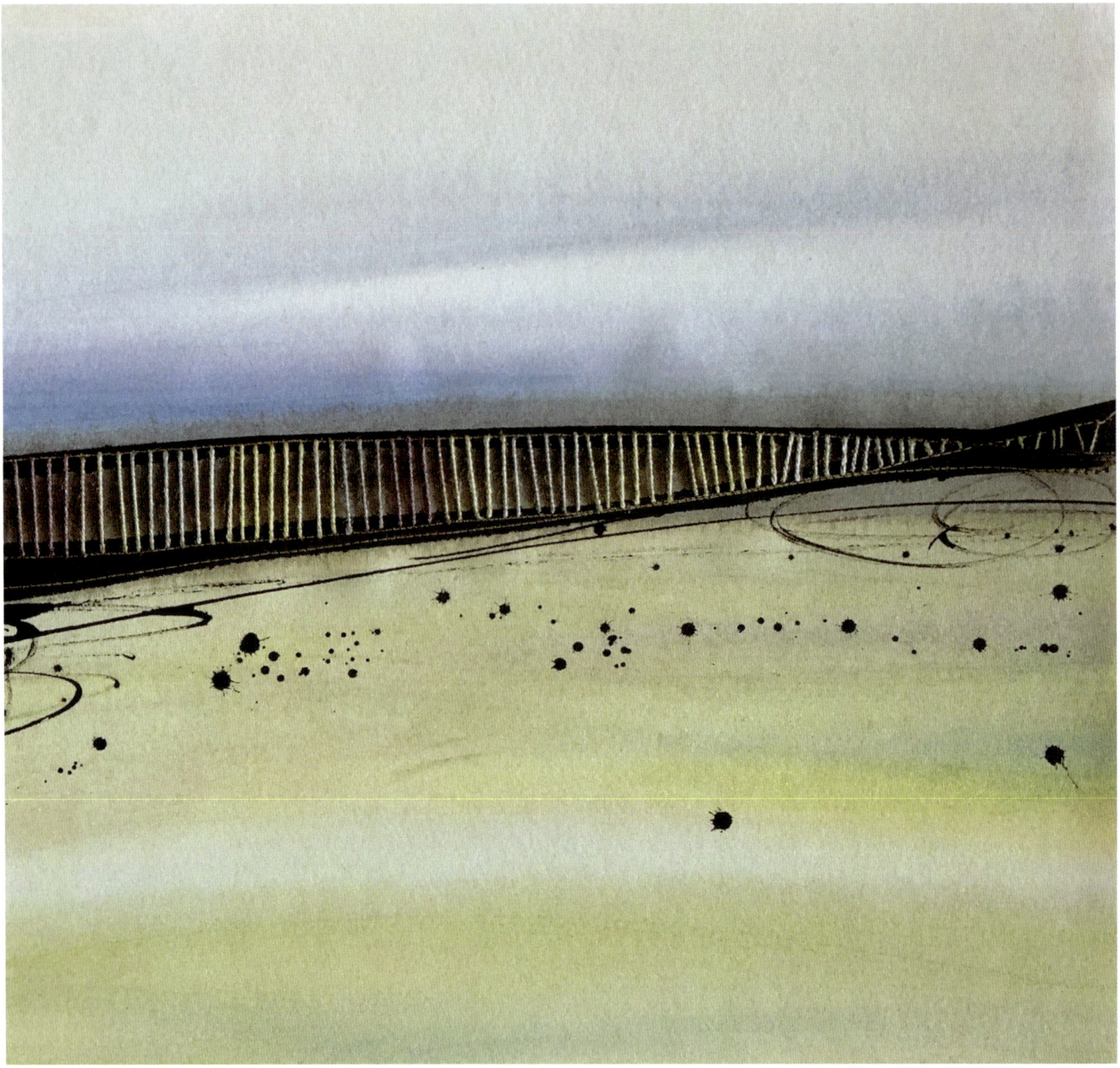

My World
Watercolor, opalescent Ink, and India ink on cotton paper with machine and hand stitch, 12" × 9" (31cm ×23cm)

INTRODUCTION

In my early 60s, I began to question the choices I had made in my life. Why had I spent so much time making art? Was it worth it? Why did I do it?

Over a five-year period, I wrote most days about what was on my mind: memories, making art, love, grief, frustrations. Like a walk through my garden, with its hidden curves and vistas, understanding the importance of making art in my life was only in my peripheral vision. Slowly, day by day, month by month, year by year, I saw how my artistic practice colored every corner of my life. Along the way, I answered those initial questions.

As I shared some of this writing with other artists, I realized that the lessons learned are more universal than I had understood. Pulling this writing together into a book was much harder than I ever imagined. As with my artwork, though, my heart led the way and kept me working at it.

May my stories help you, my reader—whether you consider yourself an artist or not—stay on course, dig deep for your own truths, and find self-knowledge in the process. I hope my experiences provide inspiration and courage for your own life journey.

For artists who read this book, I hope my frustrations and in-between times will help you stay committed to your practice until the next inspiration arrives. And may you laugh at some of my misadventures and see both the humor and courage it takes to continue your own artistic practice.

This book is organized into three sections:

- The Back Story section provides background on how I came to different art mediums and some of the most influential people in my life.
- The Infill section has snippets of what inspires me, my ways of making art and how it has woven itself into my life. This section contains essays on the flow and struggle in making art and in making a life. It is also about an artistic practice and how it illuminates life.
- The Long Walk includes sections on Parkinson's disease, hospice, and how the wisdom gained from making art has helped me rally during times of great sorrow.

With broad strokes, the answers to those initial questions are apparent in The Back Story. The Infill is full of the details. It is what gives luster to our lives; and that is where the treasure resides. The Long Walk pulls it all together.

Thank you for walking with me.

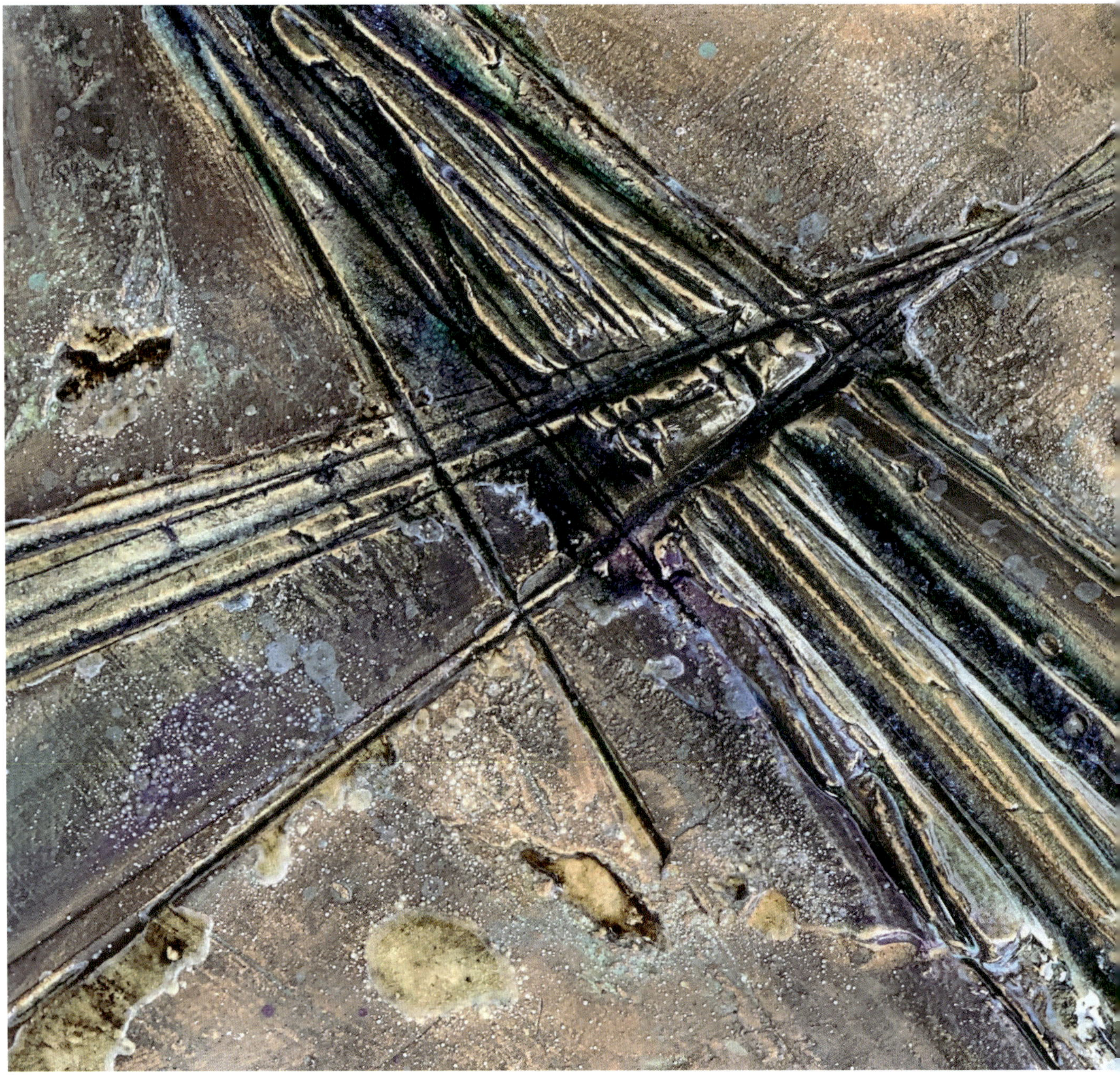

Gemstone
Stoneware tile with multiple glazes and engobes; 11" × 17.5" (28cm × 44cm)

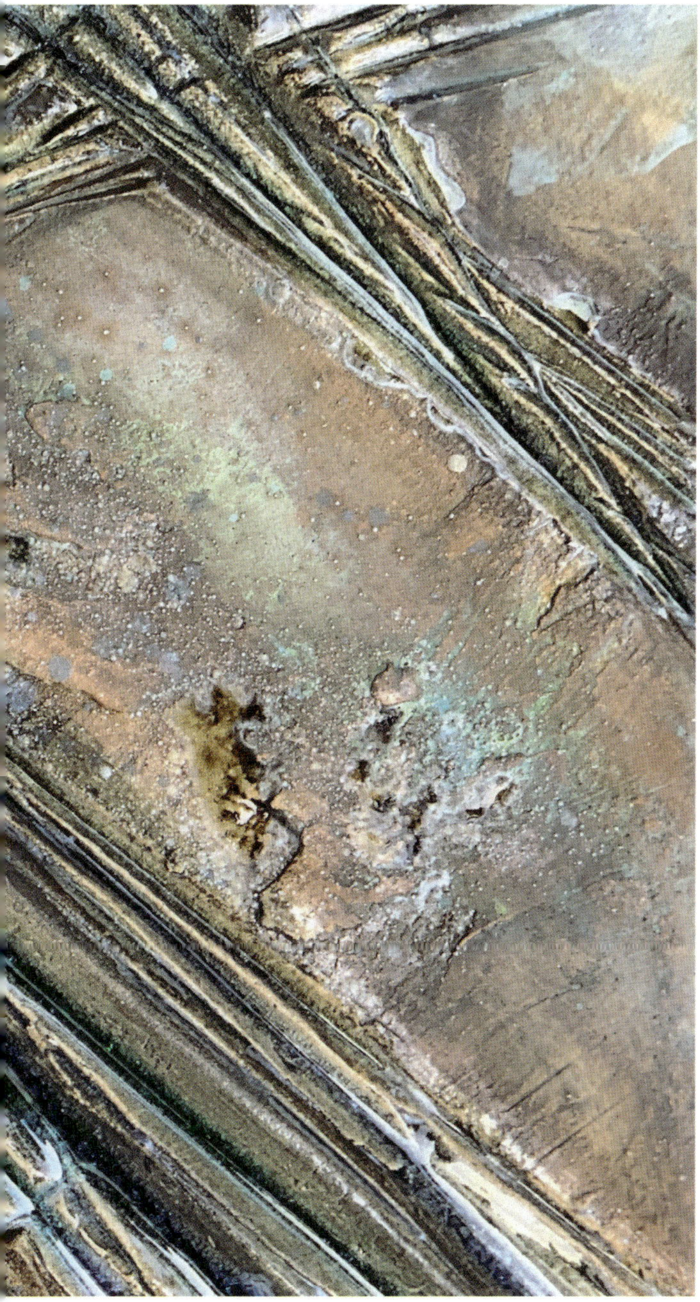

THE BACK STORY

Van Gogh • The Big Shift • Ila • The Wednesday Night Class • Tragedy • Gardens • Japan • Jean Houston • Paint • Bruce • The Barnes Foundation • Vally Always • Back to Clay • Architectural Ceramics • The Right Question • Changing Mediums

VAN GOGH

It's about 1987. I am twirling around with tears on my face in a gallery featuring Vincent van Gogh's sunflower paintings. It's the Metropolitan Museum of Art's show *Van Gogh: In Saint-Rémy and Auvers.*

Thick, textured, quick brush strokes with luscious color form the vases and flowers. The beauty of these paintings absorbs my attention and everything else around me fades.

I think to myself, *Oh, to be able to paint even one painting that is this good would make a life worthwhile. It's a worthy goal.*

Although I didn't realize it at the time, I suspect this is when it first occurred to me that I wanted to be an artist.

"Van Gogh! Are you kidding? Talk about a set-up!"

I know. It's funny, I didn't really think I could be van Gogh, but art held meaning for me. This experience has been held loosely in my memory for decades. But it's only now, that I understand its significance more fully. It happens sometimes that way, doesn't it? We remember the experience but don't fully grasp its importance.

But I am getting ahead of myself.

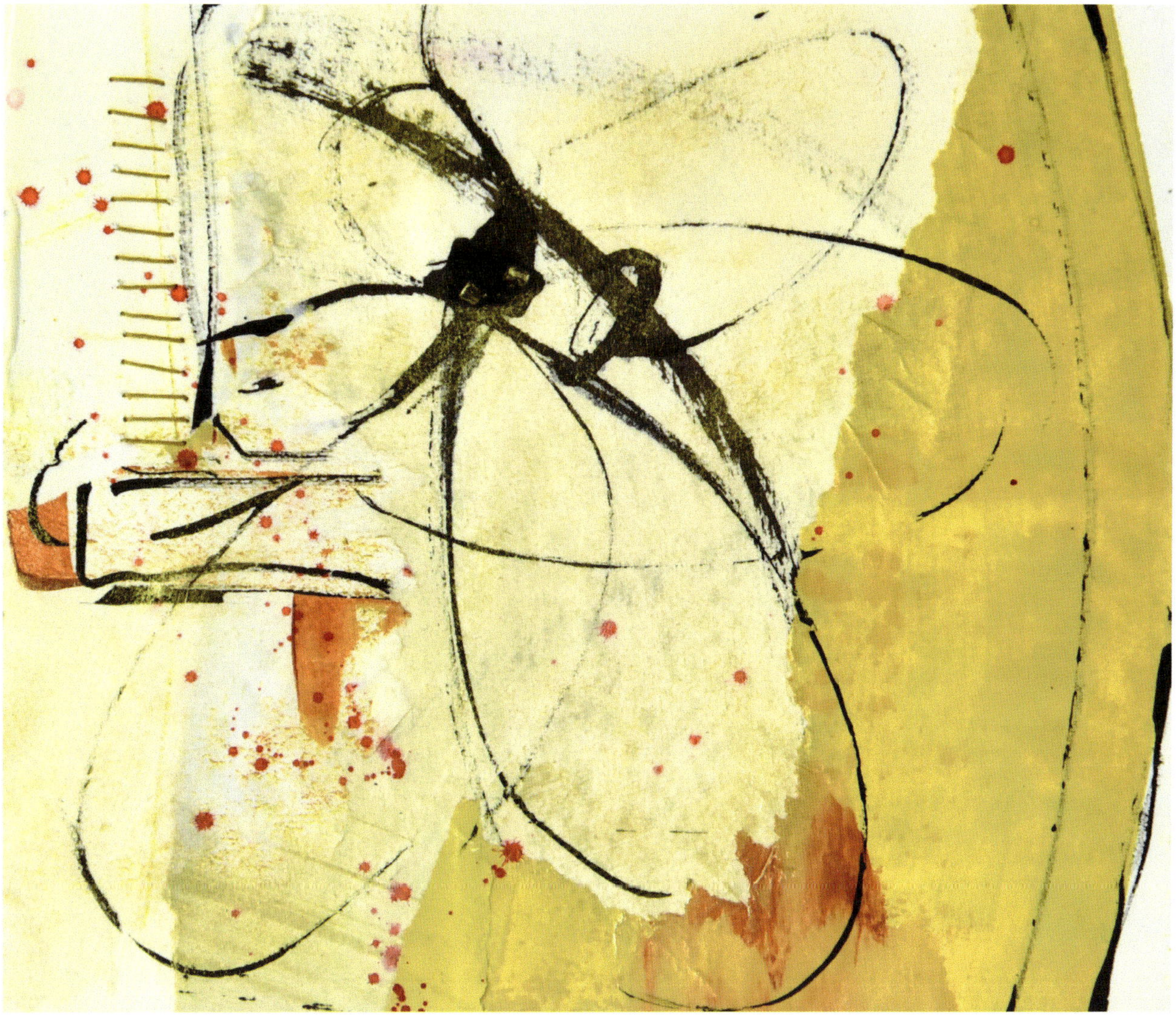

Journal page, 8" x 8" (20cm x 20cm)

THE BIG SHIFT

For years I had had the feeling that there was a whole world out there that was locked to me. I had worked for thirteen years as a bank examiner and senior bank regulator. Imagine sitting in an office with white walls, fluorescent lighting, dressed in a navy-blue suit, and looking at a stack of papers ten inches high that still required review that day. And it was already 5:00 p.m.

There were also negative undercurrents in this office: one-upmanship, gossip, jealousies, behind-the-scenes alliances, and "office politics." I hated that.

Bank examiners tend to be analytical, detail-oriented, and practical. I can be like that, too. But I was getting to know the part of me that wanted to be more eccentric, maybe even flamboyant and able to take more risks. I wanted to know different kinds of people, different occupations. I wanted to know what else was out there.

All of the above and a difficult, job-required relocation from New York City to Washington, D.C. in 1986 pushed me to take a frightening leap without a net. I left my banking career not knowing my next step.

That was certainly taking more risk.

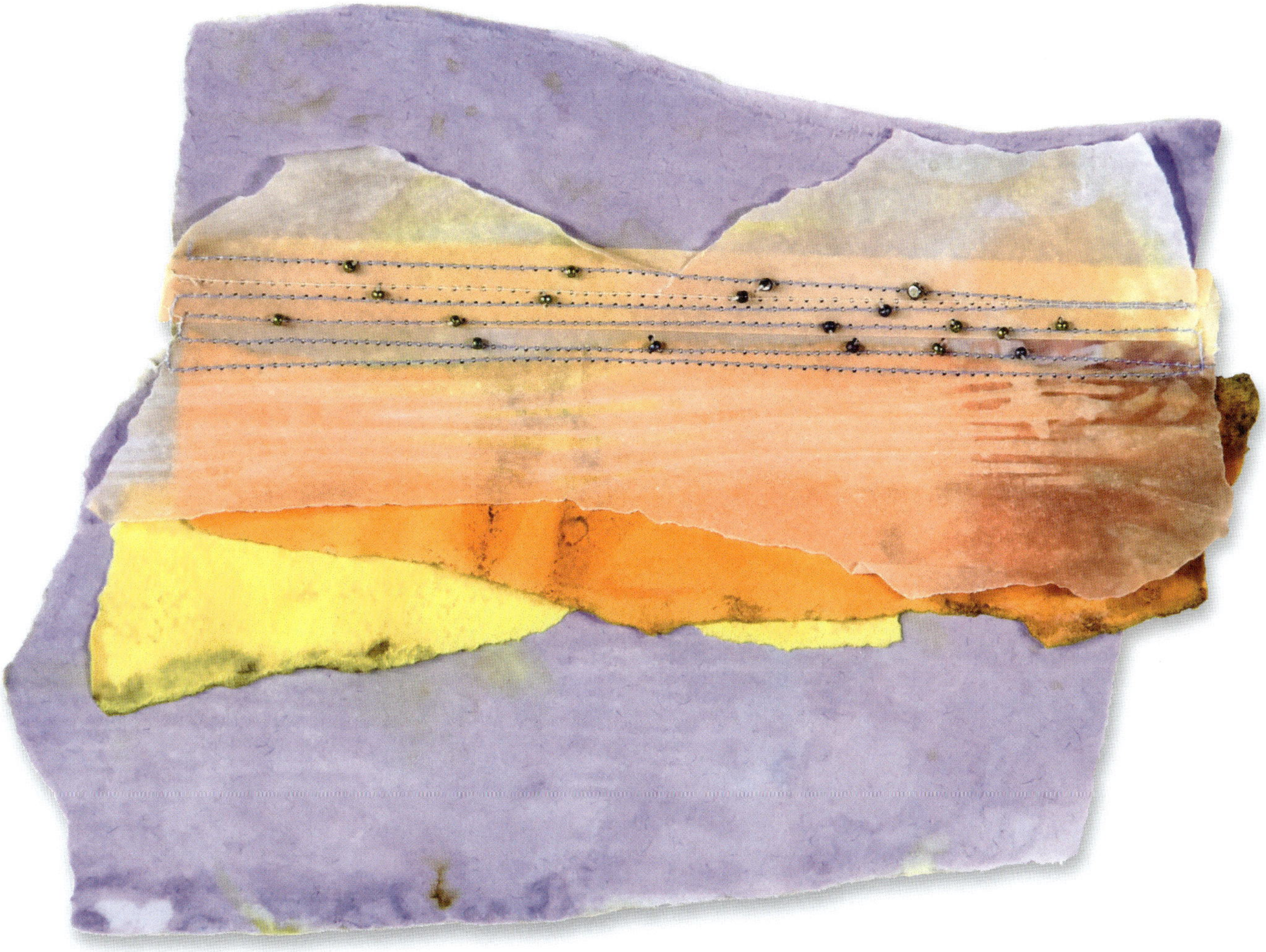

On the Water
Botanically-dyed papers with stitch and beads, 8″ x 6″ (20cm x 15cm)

I was living in New York City then (1986) and walked along the East River most sunny days. The sun glistening on the water calmed me. My mood vacillated between terror at what I had done and joy at the freedom. I wanted to learn to cook and bought Jane Brody's *Good Food* book and a few more kitchen essentials. I thought about working on a Ph.D. in psychology.

But more often than not, I went to art galleries and museums. Which is how I found myself twirling around, crying tears of joy at the Van Gogh show.

I saw his paintings just when I was wondering how I could add more meaning to my life. What did I want to do with my life?

Isn't that how it usually happens? Our most powerful experiences seem to come when we are most vulnerable, or one might say, most open and receptive to them.

I am still ahead of myself. Let me go back even further.

ILA

This new side of me I was learning about really started with a remarkable woman named Ila Gillaspie. Well, who knows an actual beginning? It's probably in our genes. But let me tell you about Ila.

There I was–in 1982 or thereabout–working with all these bank examiner/regulator types and in came Ila. She had been hired to work on the furniture design for all of the new field offices that were being set up as part of a reorganization at my office. She was from that locked world I wanted to know more about. She was creative, a risk-taker, and very funny, but she was also a hard worker, responsible, and a bit of a nudge. She was passionate about good food, pottery, and people, and ultimately, we became friends.

Ila was also a dear friend of Vally Possony, a master potter originally from Vienna, Austria and now in her 70s. Vally was a renowned potter having had a solo show at the Phillips Gallery in Washington, D. C.

Ila urged me to start taking pottery classes one night a week with Vally. She kept mentioning it to me, and I kept putting her off until one day she said, "You need to do this, Roberta. It would be good for you to do something outside of your job."

That's how I found myself driving through suburban Virginia for an interview with Vally. Vally's hidden, long, unpaved driveway opened to an oasis. It had an Asian feel–a bit Wabi-sabi–and was utterly charming.

Inside, there were floor-to-ceiling windows on two sides of a large room with views of her lush gardens. The diminutive, white-haired Vally sat behind a hand-hewn, wooden slab of a table. I later learned that Wharton Escherik, the master sculptor and wood-maker, had crafted many of the special features of the house.

But in that moment, I was only aware of the lush, tactile setting and the unusual woman scrutinizing me. It was another world away from my office with its white walls and harsh fluorescent lighting. I was there to see if I would fit in one of her pottery classes.

Vally had spread out some homemade bread, roasted peppers, and salamis served on her own handmade dishes where beauty and function blended into a harmonious whole.

"You know, I need a balance in my classes," she said finally, adding that it was a definite plus that I didn't have any prior pottery experience, because "you haven't learned any bad habits yet."

I believe we all know intuitively when we meet someone who is going to change our life. I knew that evening that my life would be altered irreversibly because of this woman.

As fate would have it, I joined her Wednesday night class without a moment of hesitation.

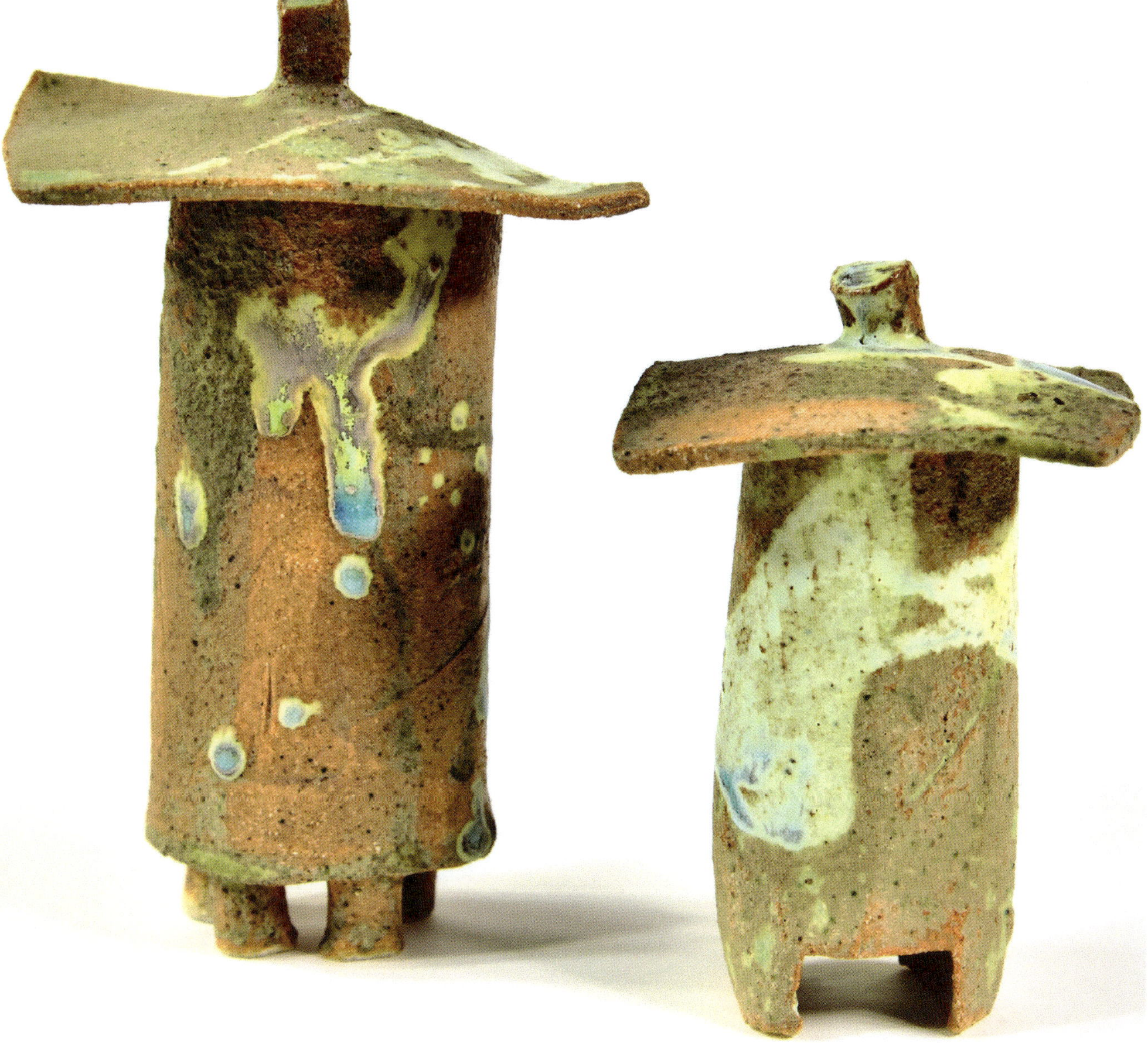

Couples
High-fired stoneware with multiple glazes

THE WEDNESDAY NIGHT CLASS

So began my years of the Wednesday night class. Vally worked in the Bernard Leach and Hamada[1] tradition, and all work was done on the wheel. Her studio was a pieced together assemblage of materials with both kick and electric wheels–maybe eight or ten in total–lined up on two sides of the room with a small walkway in between. The kick wheels, benches, shelves, and wedging boards were all framed in wood honed to a soft satin smoothness. The entire space smelled of clay and earth and had a palpable calm.

On those class nights, Vally's students–professional potters coming to gain mastery, attorneys wanting to work with their hands, political activists, and authors–arrived with covered dishes for the mid-class snack and then settled in to work. It was an odd assemblage of people who did seem to fit together and have the balance Vally wanted.

My memories of that time are still vivid: my hands first touching the rough clay, forming it into a ball, and placing it on the cold metal of the electric wheel. Then, the swirling wheel and the concentration required to center the ball of clay and begin to open it into a vessel. I especially remember the laughter and camaraderie with the other students, and Vally holding court from her chair at the end of the studio, encouraging and directing. "*Ahhhccchh . . .*" she might say, if someone was making a shape she didn't like. (Imagine the sound of someone on a roller coaster and wanting it to stop, equally sure that it would not.)

---

[1] Shoji Hamada (1894-1978) was a Japanese ceramic artist who produced handmade, functional vessels.

I also remember Vally, head tilted quizzically to the side with eyes closed, holding a pot to examine it and learn it first from her fingertips. When she made pots, she did it first from feel, not sight. Her fingermarks embedded in her pots followed the circular pull of the wheel and seemed to pass to the holder her tactile awareness and gift of touch.

In those years, my own sense of touch expanded. I could feel a tingling in my fingertips when they brushed linen or silk or clay or fired pottery. Now, that tingling in my fingertips is a sign to me that my hands are ready to take over; I should quiet my mind and let my fingertips govern movement for a while.

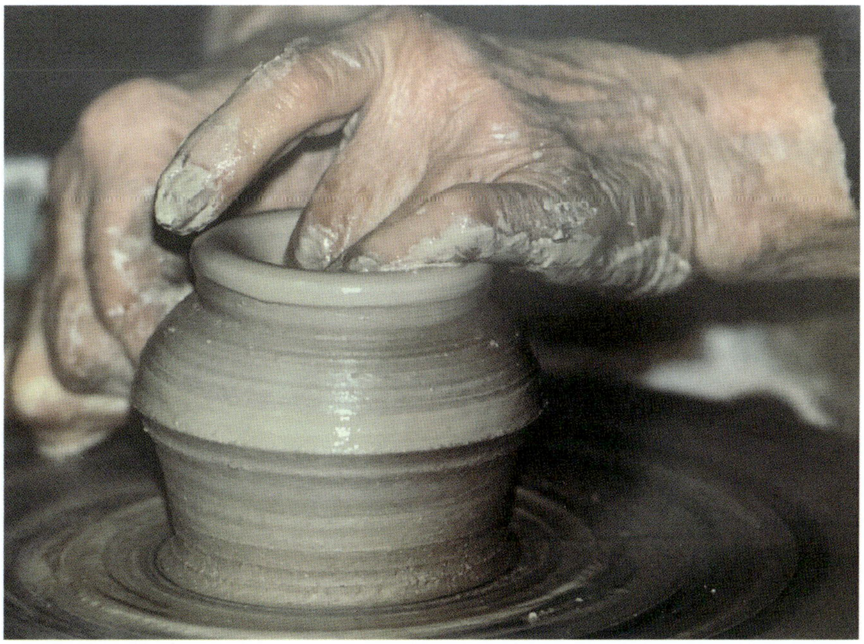

Vally's hands. Photographer unknown.

TRAGEDY

While I knew that my friend Ila suffered from terrible asthma, I didn't fully grasp the risk until the day that she suddenly died. It was a terrible blow to both Vally and me, and I began to visit Vally more often outside of class in an attempt to soothe our own and one another's grief.

Food was almost always a centerpiece of these visits. One time, Vally made a cabbage-broth soup with a piece of mortadella Italian sausage laid across the top and served it in one of her soup bowls. It was magnificent. Another time, brown and wild rice, wheat berries, and spiced sausage with onion and peppers were stir-fried with an unusual blend of seasonings. "I cook each vegetable separately to keep the flavors distinct," Vally would say. I began to notice the pleasure derived from knowing how food is prepared and where it comes from.

While we ate, Vally would show me things: a particularly beautiful green pepper full of shadings and curves, fresh mâche lettuce from her garden ("It's the best. They don't sell it here."), or a spoon expertly carved from a gnarled piece of wood brought to her by a student "with taste." Another time, she laid out four different pears so I could taste the difference and know for myself which to buy.

Because Vally enjoyed all living things so much, I, too, found myself on the lookout for unusual, interesting, or beautiful things. I started to notice rocks, wildflowers, and insects. I went to farmers markets where the produce would likely be more unusual and interesting, less antiseptic. I started to more closely notice plants and trees. I began to bring Vally some of the things I found most interesting, like a macadamia nut from Hawaii still in its shell. All the while, of course, my own vision of the world was changing.

In retrospect, she had become an "aesthetics mentor" to me, teaching me much more than how to make pottery. A whole new realm of noticing–the beautiful, the ugly, the sublime–opened up to me in relation to nature and man-made works of art.

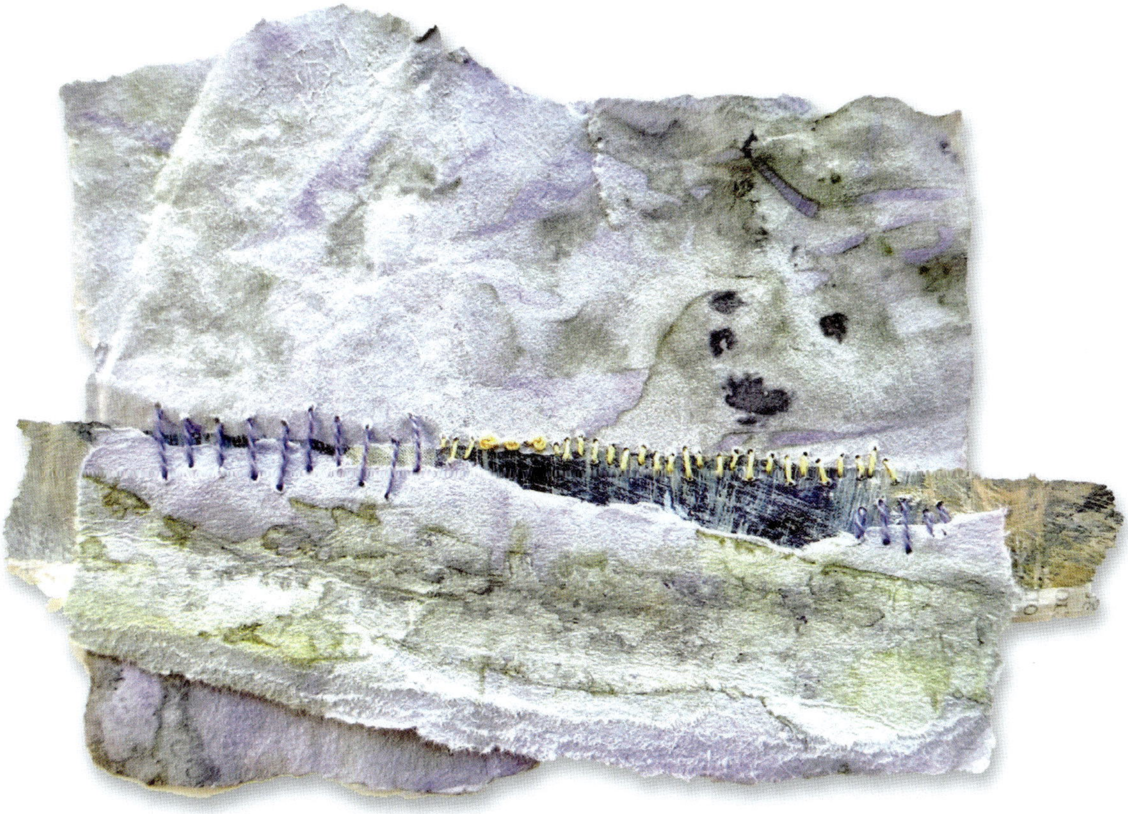

Stormy Weather
Collage with washi paper and stitch, 5" x 4" (13cm x 10cm)

GARDENS

My experiences with Vally and clay began to remind me of my childhood connection to the land, a connection that had been fraying while working in an office.

My mom's dad, Grandpi Silvis, had a vegetable garden that covered an acre (or so it seems to me now) at "the lake" near Maple Lake in Minnesota. I remember walking the rows with him each morning as we inspected what was growing well and what needed a little help. His kindness and interest in the land seeped into my being and is still with me.

Then there was my Grandma's cottage flower garden outside my Wagner grandparents' farmhouse near Fairfax, Minnesota. She had a huge vegetable garden, too, but it was the cottage garden that captured my attention. She'd scoff at it. "Oh, yeah . . . I don't know," she'd say, shrugging off its beauty and importance. I wish I could remember what she had planted there, but, instead of the specifics, I remember the riotous interplay of color and texture. And I see her unacknowledged need to create beauty and how that has been carried down through the generations to me.

Of course, Vally had a garden, too. Like many Japanese-style homes, there was no indication from the street of the beautiful grounds and charming home tucked away. I remember the day she called to say, in her Viennese accent, "You must come, *Ro-bear-tah*! The Lychoris are blooming everywhere, and there's a sea of pink in the front yard."

When I lived on 93rd and Lexington in New York City, I'd skirt Central Park most days on my walk to and from work on 46th and Avenue of the Americas. Central Park is a big part of why I loved Manhattan so much. Then, as now, I applaud the vision, the courage, and the persistence it took to create that park.

And whenever I could, I made my own gardens. Some were tiny, some were just a little patch here or there. Many never met my vision, but once in a while there was success, such as the time I got the Scarlet Runner Beans growing up the side of a rectory in Warrenton, Virginia. Oh, they were a vision. Or the big patch of blooming delphiniums I could see outside my window there. No wonder people go nuts over delphiniums.

As I think about this now, how could I possibly have spent so many long days in an office building with so little connection to nature? What made me think I could?

JAPAN

Thinking about gardens, I am reminded of my 1979 trip to Japan as a young bank examiner to examine the Tokyo branch of a New York-based multinational bank. The US embassy had a business relationship with the Okura Hotel, one of the most beautiful hotels in Tokyo, and, as a result, I got to stay there.

I sat in the Okura Hotel lobby every Saturday morning when the *ikebana* master arrived to change the huge central flower arrangement. She was a tiny woman, probably in her 70s, white hair in a low bun, dressed in a kimono. She would carefully pick up a cherry branch and examine it so closely that I could feel her concentration clear across the lobby. Then she would effortlessly place it in the receptacle and move on to the next piece. In a fairly short time, she arranged the branches into a lyrical dance of cherry blossoms. I had never seen anything so beautiful. It was like observing a Japanese precursor to Vally.

Much of that trip was, by necessity, taken up with going to work—in another sterile office building—and doing what examiners do. However, one weekend I was able to go to the ancient city of Kyoto and commune with its miraculous gardens during cherry blossom time. The experience is still with me today. In Japan, gardening is considered one of the traditional arts and is revered along with tea ceremony, calligraphy, and architecture. How could anyone doubt the artistry in those gardens? I still have images of moss growing on stones and tree roots polished to satin peeking up through the paths.

Looking back, how could I think that my love of beauty and gardens had started with Ila? It was already in my genes; she just reminded me of that connection. Some people do that for us; they remind us of who we are and who we are meant to be.

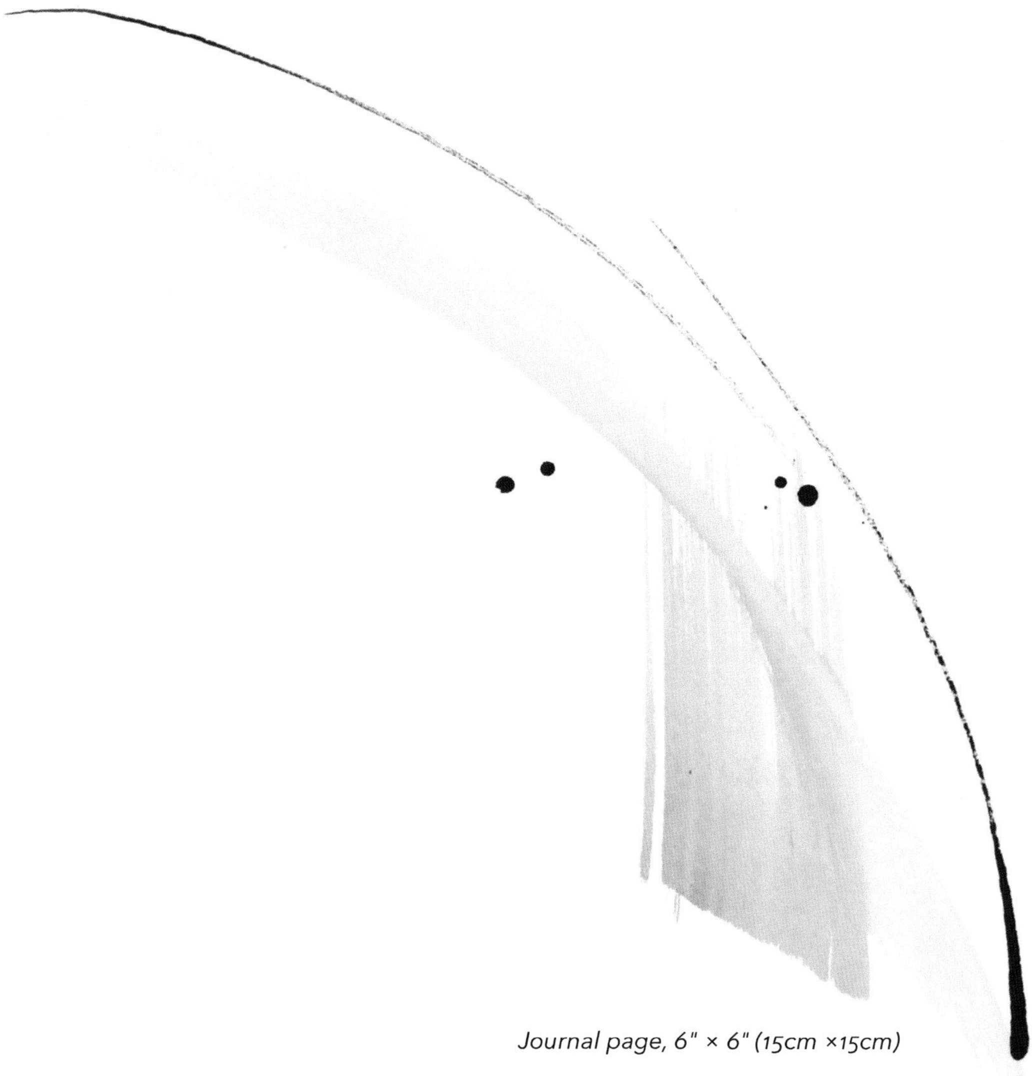

Journal page, 6" × 6" (15cm ×15cm)

JEAN HOUSTON

While I was unemployed and wandering around New York City, I heard about Dr. Jean Houston's Mystery School. I don't remember what drew me to that school, but I do remember reading or hearing the words "body, mind, and soul," and I was drawn to those words.

It was a bold move to sign up for Jean's Mystery School, but I was in a risk-taking mood. It entailed driving to upstate New York for nine weekends to think about things as far away from banking as they could be: mythology, history, the great saints, my own inner longings, and my path moving forward.

Those inspiring, transformative weekends were filled with singing, dancing, and contemplation, and Jean always assigned homework for the intervening month. One time, we were to read Cervantes' Don Quixote and then each day write the story of our day from the perspective of the novel's main characters, Sancho Panza and Don Quixote. The daily telling of my story from those two perspectives helped me to see that there are many different ways to interpret life's events.

I met so many wonderful artists, thinkers, and writers at Mystery School, and, through my interactions with them, I began to discover a larger world. At the same time, those nine months opened me up to my own inner self and steadied me from the emotional roller coaster of daily life. Since that time, whenever I experience a challenging series of events, I tell or write the story of that day or week from the perspectives of both the optimistic Don Quixote and the worrying Sancho Panza. It's helpful.

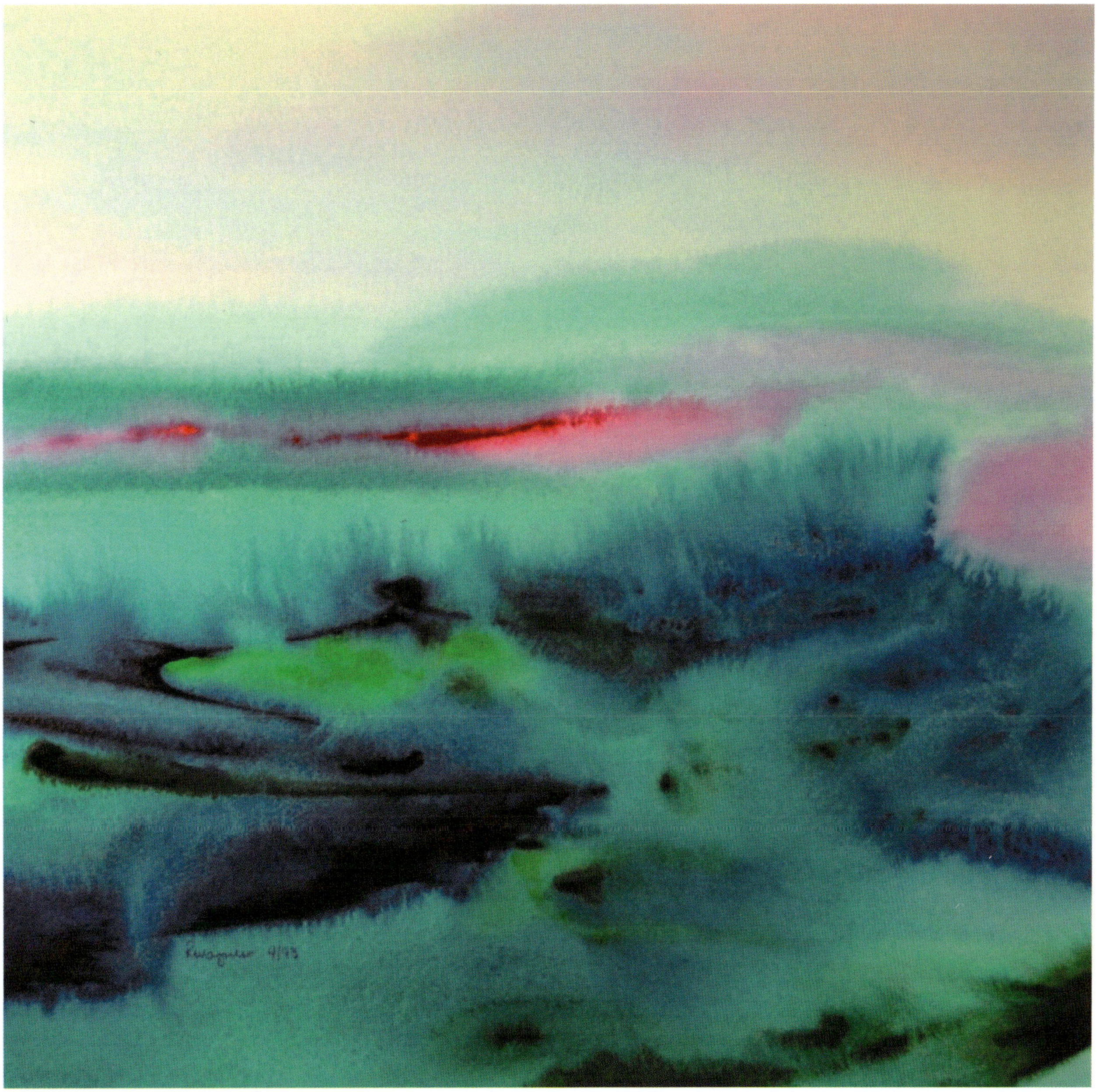

Cape Cod
Water media on Arches paper, 21" × 21" (53cm ×53cm)

PAINT

As often happens with mentors and their students, Vally's views on pottery began to seem too limiting to me. I loved the work of Toshiko Takaezu. I could feel the power in the ceramic sculptures of Peter Voulkos. Vally didn't always approve. For her, pottery—she never called it ceramics—had to be functional. I was veering away from that.

I had so much loyalty to Vally, though, that I didn't want to go in a different direction with clay, so I turned to paint. Wandering around art museums in New York City and Washington, D.C., I fell in love with the work of Helen Frankenthaler, Morris Louis, Mark Rothko, Richard Diebenkorn, and others—especially the abstract expressionists. I wanted to try it and wondered how hard it could be.

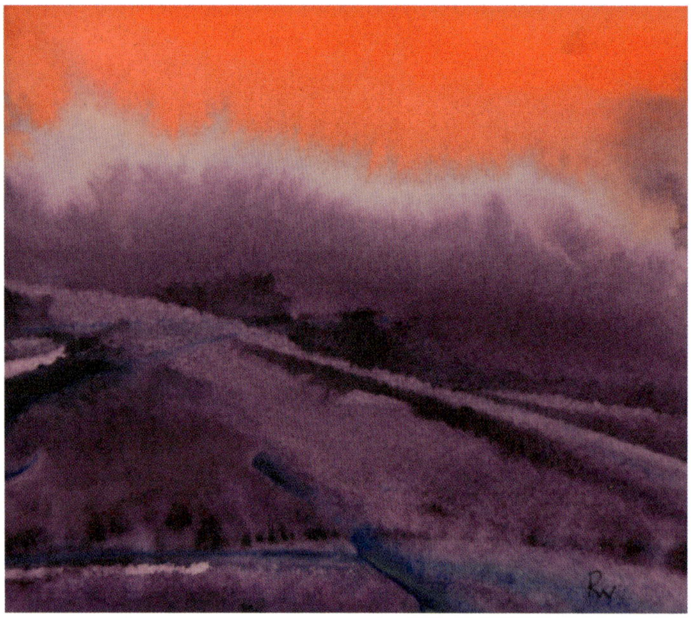

Small piece cut from a larger failed painting.

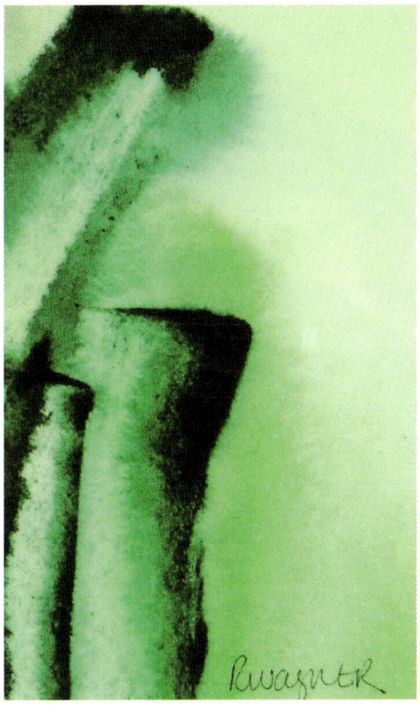

Small piece cut from a larger failed painting.

So, without having a clue about painting materials or techniques, I went to Utrecht Art Supply Store in Washington, D.C. I felt like a stealth buyer of art supplies and didn't want to ask for help from the clerks because they all felt like "real artists." I bought expensive 24" × 36" (61 cm × 91 cm) Arches cotton paper, brushes, watercolors, opalescent inks, and acrylics.

I brought my stash home and couldn't wait to try it out. I had a glass dining room table at one end of the living room in my small apartment. I carefully taped plastic all over the floor and laid the paper on the table to begin.

At first, it was magical! Colors washed across the paper, and I loved seeing them blend together. But, "Uh-oh . . . red and green made a very yucky brown," I thought. "Uh-oh . . . I don't like red and blue together." So, I sat down in my comfy chair discouraged. After sitting there a few minutes, I was so frustrated to have wasted my expensive paper that I grabbed the paper, ran to the shower, and put the paper under the water.

What do you know? I had some charming little fragments that I loved. The overall composition was a mess, but there were some sections that had movement and charm. I started cutting up the paper to find the little jewels within.

So began my love affair with small art.

We just never know what's going to happen when we dive into something new, especially when it turns out to be much harder than we ever thought it would be.

BRUCE

By 1987, I had taken six months off work and moved back to Washington, D. C. from New York City to take another position as a senior savings and loan regulator. I know . . . another office job! I sometimes have to do things twice before I learn.

It's no big surprise, I guess, that I only stayed in that position for a couple of years. Instead, I thought I would try to be a bank consultant (the standard out-of-work position) until I could figure out "what I really wanted to do." So, a little like when I decided to try painting, I just jumped in and thought I could somehow make it work.

I knew that to be successful in this new endeavor I needed to network, and fortunately, as has happened at other times in my life, someone came to my rescue. In early 1989, I met Bruce Bugbee, who had managed a large group of financial institution consultants for a national firm for twenty years. He, too, had taken the bold step of leaving the big firm to go out on his own. When I met him, he was part of a loose partnership that had formed an umbrella company to do bank consulting. He understood the value of getting an outside opinion, how to tackle gnarly problems, and how to provide temporary, expert assistance.

He taught me how to be a real consultant: how to go into an organization and look at the dynamics with clear-sightedness. He taught me how to deliver tough-but-needed news to a client, how to look for creative solutions, and how to use a whole host of tools and techniques to approach different problems. Along the way, I realized that being a consultant was a good fit for me. I liked being able to step outside the dynamics of an organization to see where I might be able to insert a tweak or two that would help improve the lives of those working within it.

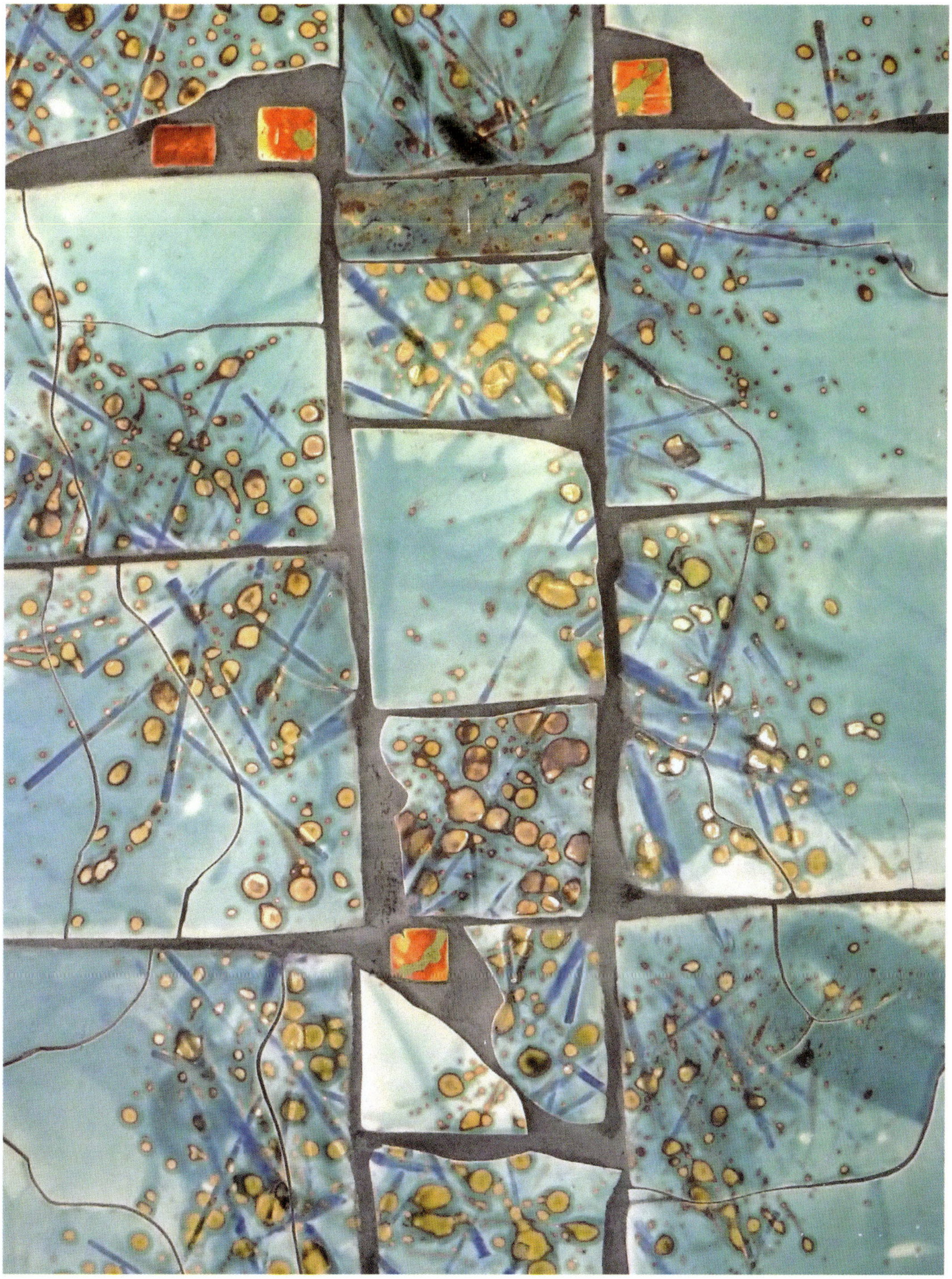

Abstracted Garden: A Collaboration
I originally made these 12" x 12" (30cm × 30cm) tiles for a fireplace surround but they cracked in the firing. I was ready to throw them out when Bruce decided to assemble them into a collage. I added the small orange tiles. 24" x 31" (61cm × 79cm).

Our combined experience worked well to help banks in crisis, and we ended up working on several engagements together. We also became friends and found it easy to talk and laugh together. He knew how to take breaks so that work wasn't all-consuming (something I have never been very good at). And he loved art, so we went to museums and galleries wherever we were for business. He had a great eye and was able to analyze light, line, color, and composition better than I was. My reaction to art was, and still is, more emotional.

I always took anyone I was seeing to meet Vally, hoping for her approval. So far, everyone had been rejected as not good enough. Finally, in 1992, as my friendship with Bruce moved to more than friendship, I took Bruce to meet her. Her eyes sparkled, and she said, "Yes, he's quite nice." Of course, by then, her opinion would not have mattered to me, but I was relieved she liked him, too.

We were married in January of 1994. We were such an unlikely couple; Bruce was eighteen years older than me, for one thing. That's a big thing, and the older we got the bigger it became. But it's an even bigger thing to find someone who will always listen to you with their heart open, wanting the best for you and respecting you in the process. With Bruce, I found a way to have more freedom in my work life so that I could have time for art and gardens and cooking.

We had both taken crooked and circuitous paths in life and, fortunately, found each other.

THE BARNES FOUNDATION

In 1993, before Bruce and I married, I was considering going to law school knowing it would help my consulting practice. But then a friend told me about The Barnes Foundation in Philadelphia, which includes a vast art collection and an educational institution. The Barnes, as it is familiarly known, was founded in 1922 by Dr. Albert C. Barnes, who knew a lot about art. Imagine . . . he amassed the largest collection of the great painters of his era (Matisse, Van Gogh, Cézanne, Renoir) when those paintings could be purchased for a song.

Instead of law school, I signed up for the art education program at The Barnes and took a train from Washington, D.C., to Philadelphia one day a week for the next two years. Often in the decades since, I have sighed, then laughed, over the impracticality of that decision. Clearly, my heart, not my head, was taking the lead.

Dr. Barnes had developed a theory of art, a way to look at it and analyze its qualities. His theories are complex, and his writing is obtuse. However, I know that if I had thoroughly mined his writings, I would know a lot more about art than I do now.

Still, a few of his concepts stuck with me and are powerful explanations of why some art stays with us and touches us deeply. "Transferred value" is one of those concepts, which can best be described by using examples. In class, for instance, we looked at a lovely little painting of a vase with red and orange flowers by Renoir. It had the feeling—or transferred value—of the sun on a bright, gorgeous day. This little painting was more than a vase of flowers. It was the sun; it was joy.

In another example, the paintings of Gustav Klimt—including his famous painting Woman in Gold—often have a transferred value of jewels or a jewel box. Woman in Gold is not just a painting of a woman; it reminds us of a treasure trove of jewels.

The class was a gift to my eyes and myself. Sometimes impractical decisions, with our hearts in the lead, are exactly the way to go.

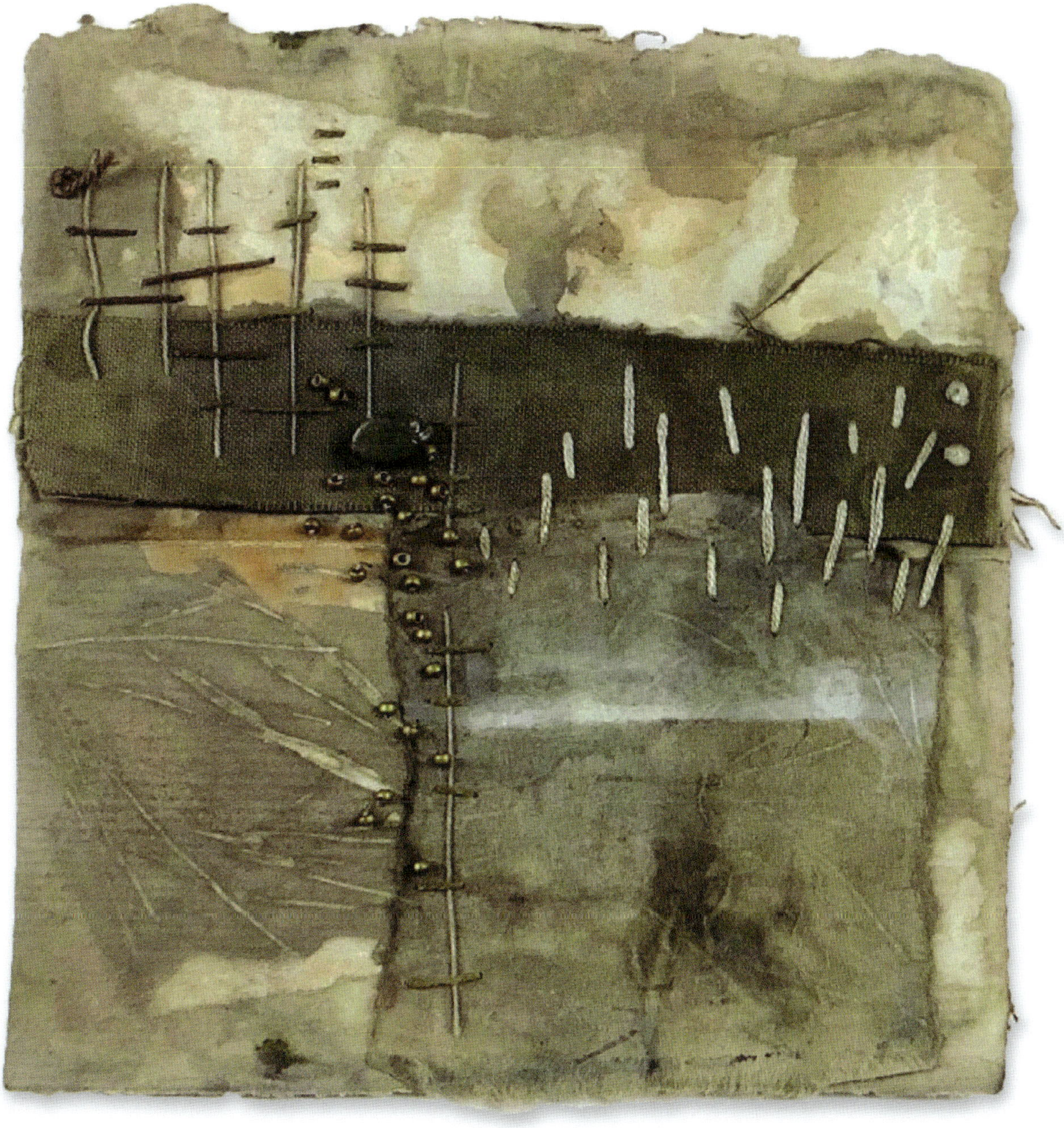

Remnants
This has a transferred value of something buried and brought to light, something old, something with a history.
Botanically-dyed papers and fabrics with stitch and beads, 5" × 5" (13cm ×13cm)

VALLY ALWAYS

Through the years, I would see Vally and sometimes throw pots with her, but I didn't show her what I was painting. I was painting a lot. Bruce helped me set up a studio in the lower level of our townhome in D.C., and I was preparing for a gallery show of the paintings. When I finally dared to show Vally my paintings, I was relieved when she said that she loved them.

In 1994, we had a harsh winter in Washington; it was bitter cold, and ice covered everything. I went to class after a particularly harsh storm and was startled when I saw her. Her heating had failed, and she seemed to have aged years overnight. It was too much for her, and she died a few months later.

Even now, decades after her death, I wonder at the miracle of being introduced to her and think about all of the ways her mentorship and friendship changed me. She was a role model for a life I knew I wanted to live. Naively, I didn't realize then what exactly would be required to make the shift to a life more like hers. Bumps in the road and challenges in life continued, as they always do. But now, when I look at my home and garden, I see remnants of her influence everywhere.

The people we have loved do live on in us long after their deaths.

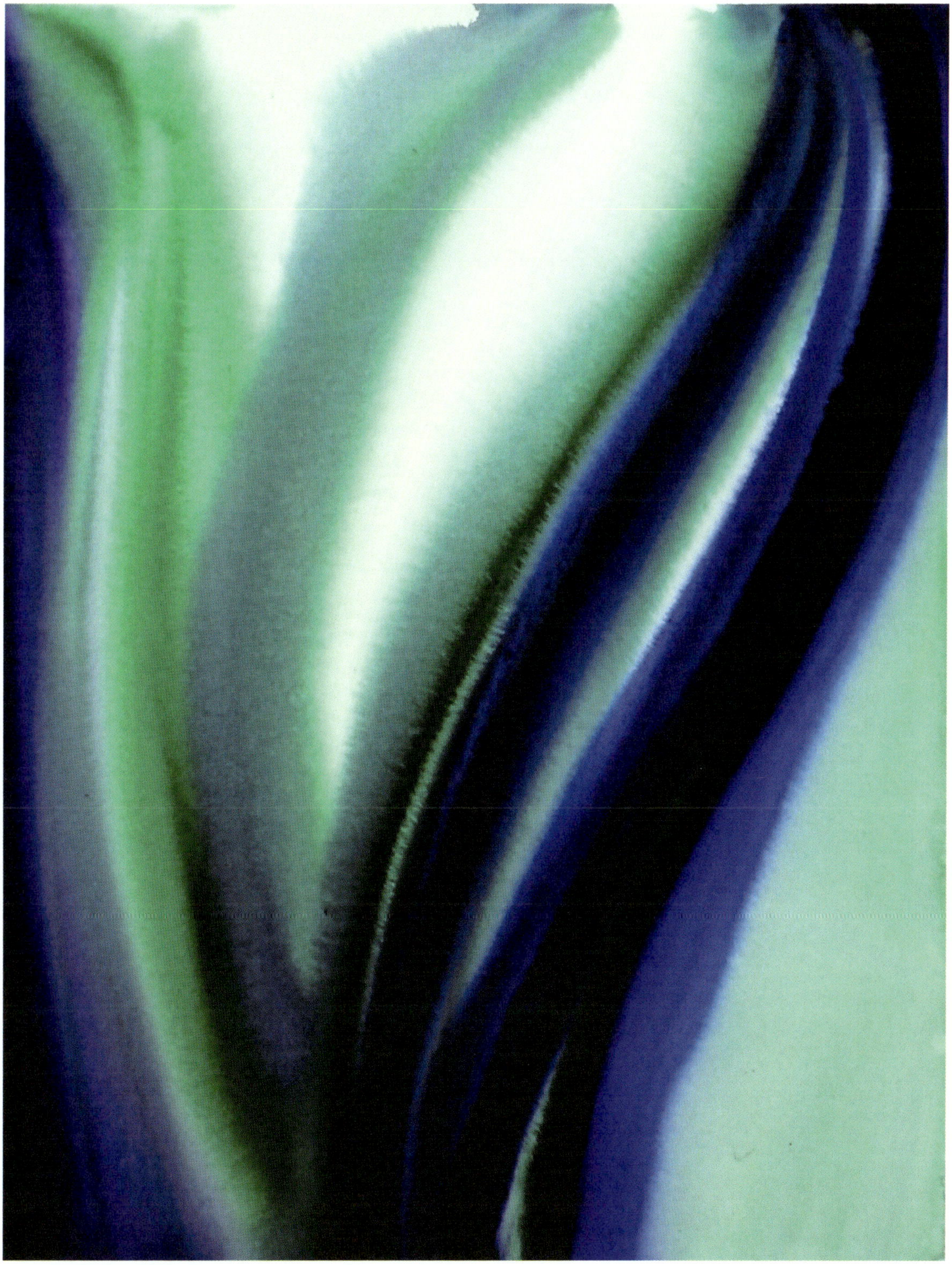

Growth
One of my first paintings
Water media on Arches paper, 21" × 30" (53cm ×76cm)

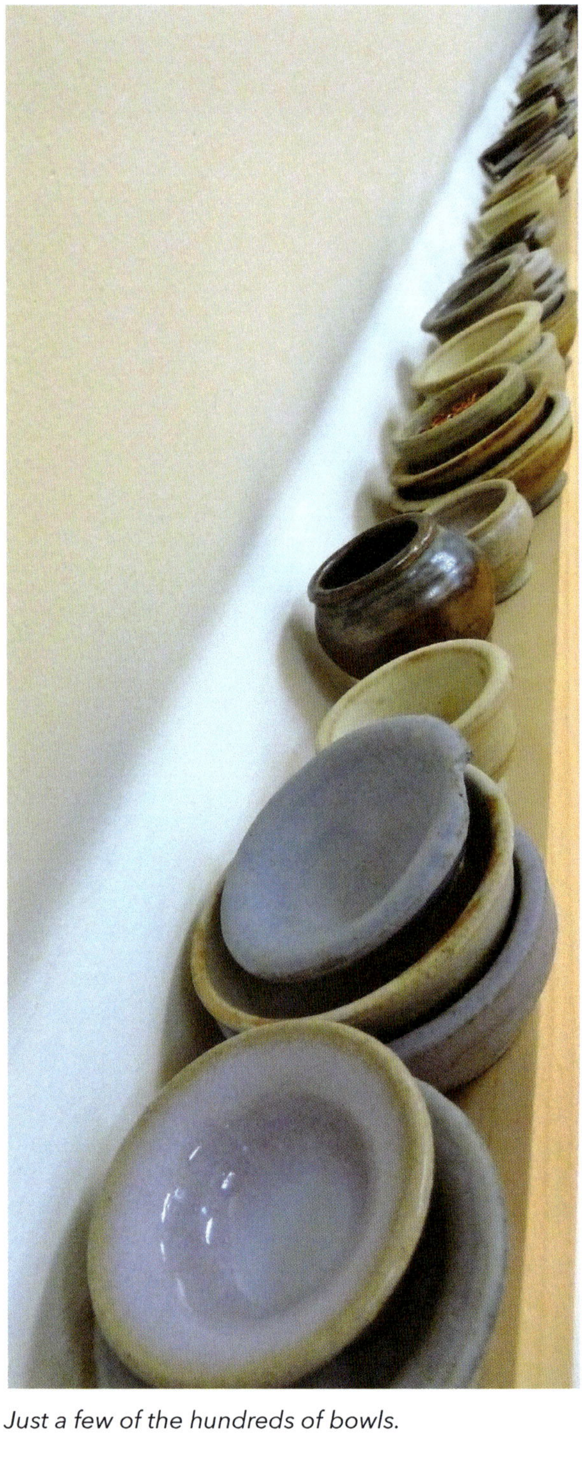

Just a few of the hundreds of bowls.

BACK TO CLAY

After Vally passed away, I eventually went back to clay. I wanted to make huge architectural ceramic pieces with interesting, rich glazes. Such glazes are most easily obtained in a gas or wood kiln. But for large pieces, I needed to use an electric kiln to gain some consistency. How, I wondered, could I recreate these mesmerizing glazes in an electric kiln? So began an intensive study of glaze chemistry.

I wasn't trying to create a specific glaze; I was trying to understand what would happen to a surface if I changed one ingredient. I wanted to be like a cook who adds a dash of this and a dash of that to create the desired effect.

I started throwing little bowls and making glaze tests. I think I had accumulated about three hundred bowls when I knew I had to find another way or the bowls would overtake me. However, the little bowls were charming. I made each one different, often carving the foot and trying to make it special. I loved these little bowls and still have thirty of them left. It was hard to part with the other two hundred and seventy, but I think they went to good homes.

Finally, I started making test tiles; Bruce was my enabler. He mounted my tiles on beautiful 24″ × 36″ (61cm × 91cm) maple boards, and by the time I finally quit making them, I had eighteen boards. Today I have only six left, all of which are still hanging in our home. It has been hard for me to part with the others; however, I sold a few and donated the rest of them to a school.

The truth is that I had learned enough to accomplish my mission after the first six tile boards. Looking back, though, those tile boards were my art during that time. I love them and the story they tell.

Now I think of them as "surprise art." Sometimes we don't understand the significance of what we're doing until years later. I was following my heart; it never leads me too far off course.

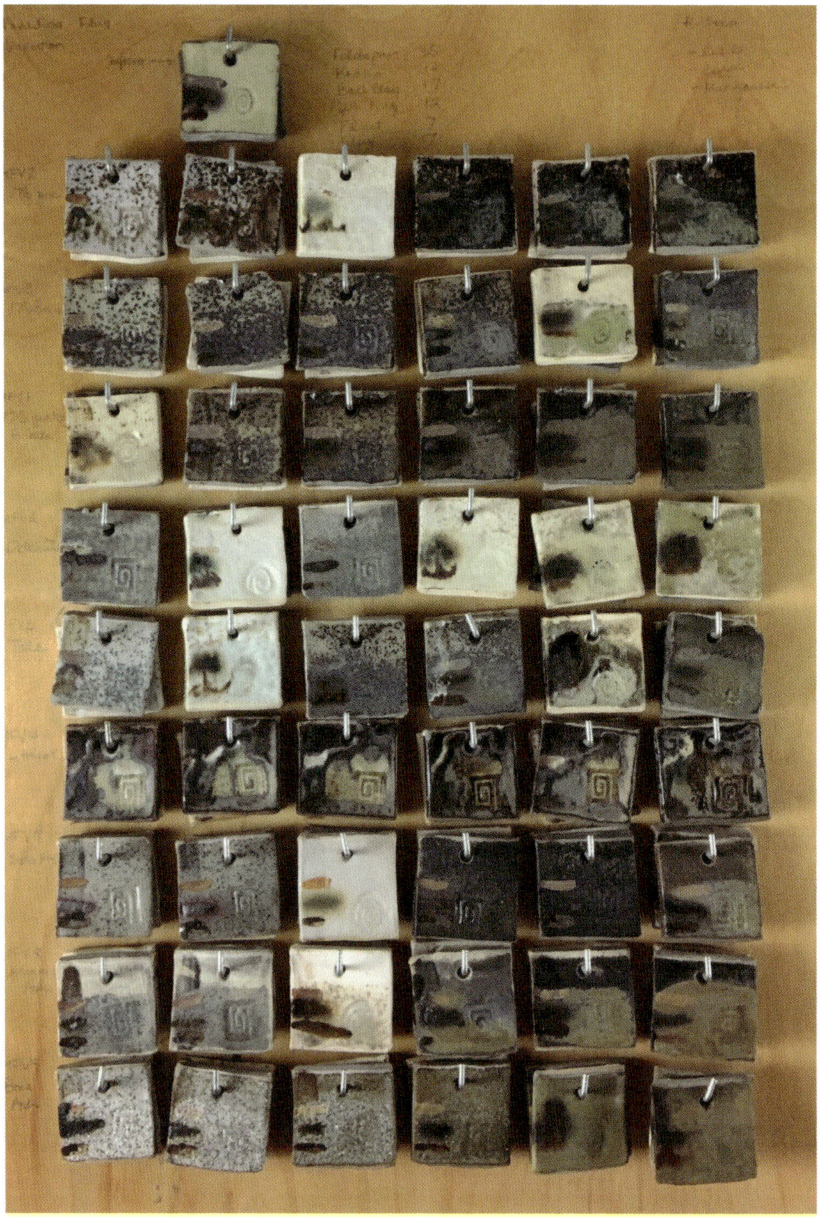

Sample glaze study board

ARCHITECTURAL CERAMICS

I went on to work with architectural ceramics for years. My largest commission was an eight-foot diameter fountain for the Lewis Ginter Botanical Garden in Richmond, Virginia. One of my favorite pieces from this time period was a maquette I made for a possible commission for a meditative nave at the Washington National Cathedral. It was 13' (4m) long and about 3' (1m) wide. Bruce assembled it into three sections that represented the Earth moving to sky then moving to the heavens. I still have the Earth section, and a friend has the other two.

The maquette made use of all my glaze studies as I used various clays, glazes, slips, and engobes to get the effect I was looking for. Fortunately, the Washington National Cathedral did not proceed with the project; I don't know how I would have made the thousands of tiles required. But I love these three pieces.

So often I am saved from myself.

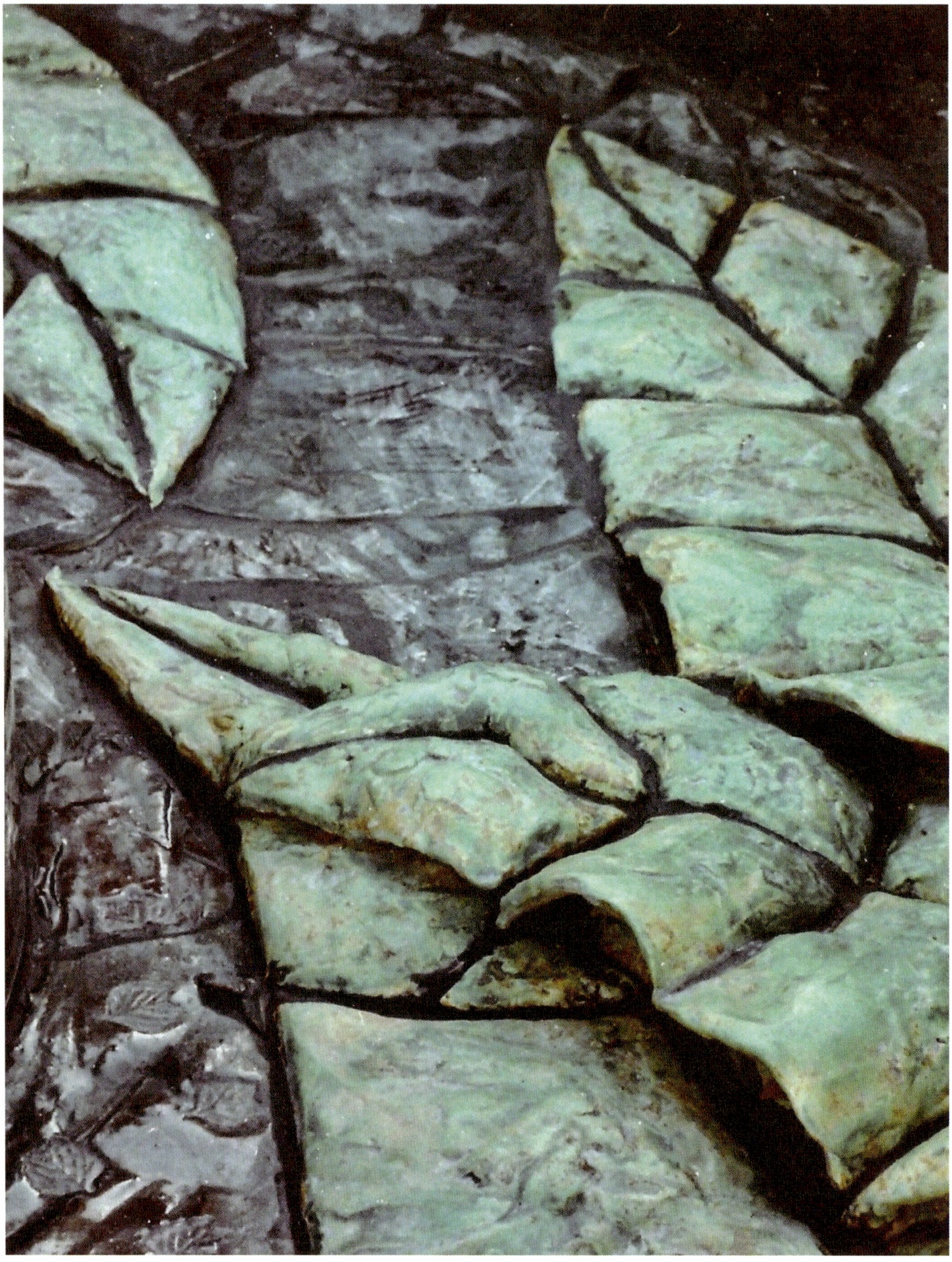

The fountain for the Lewis Ginter Botanical Garden in Richmond, VA

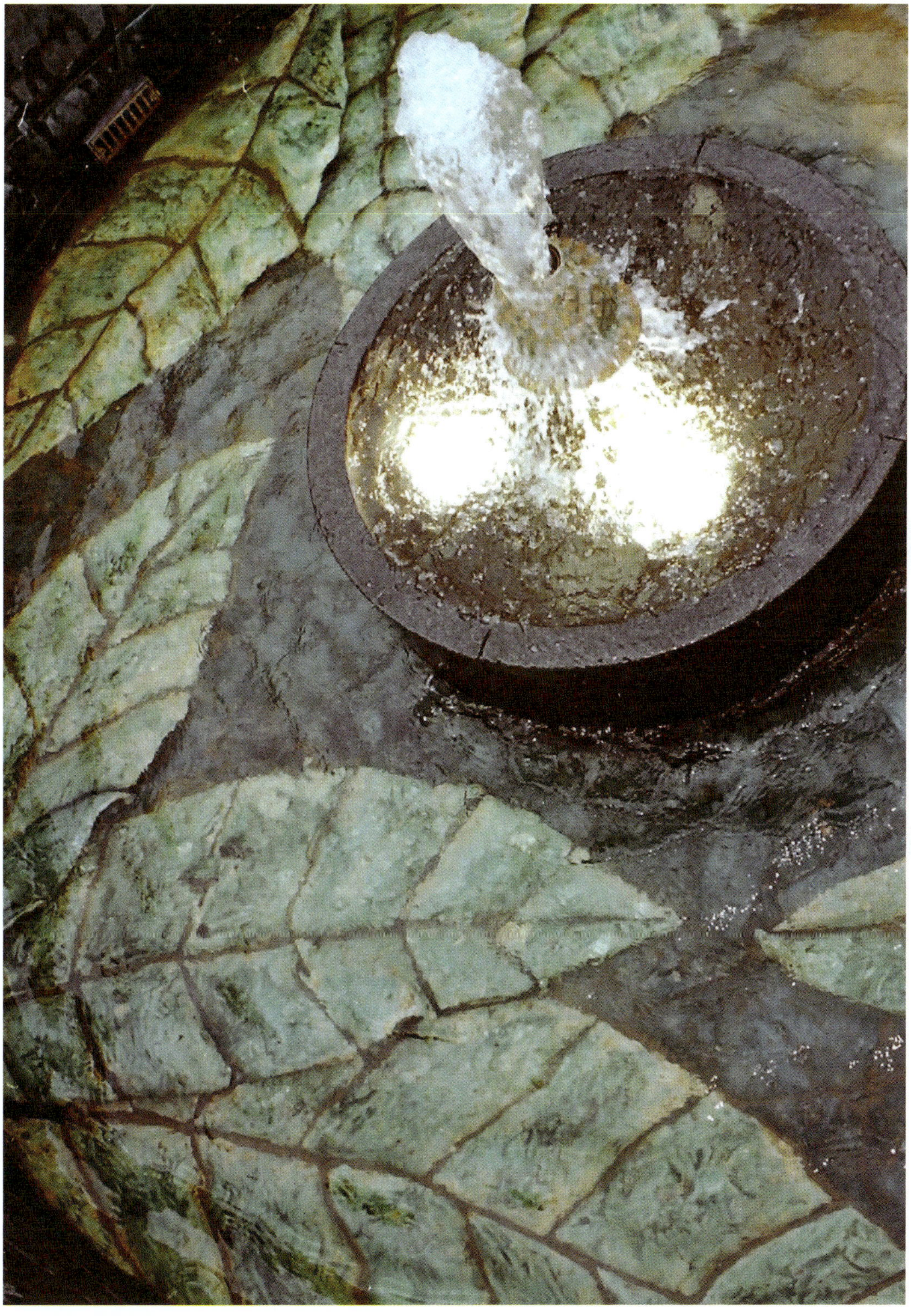

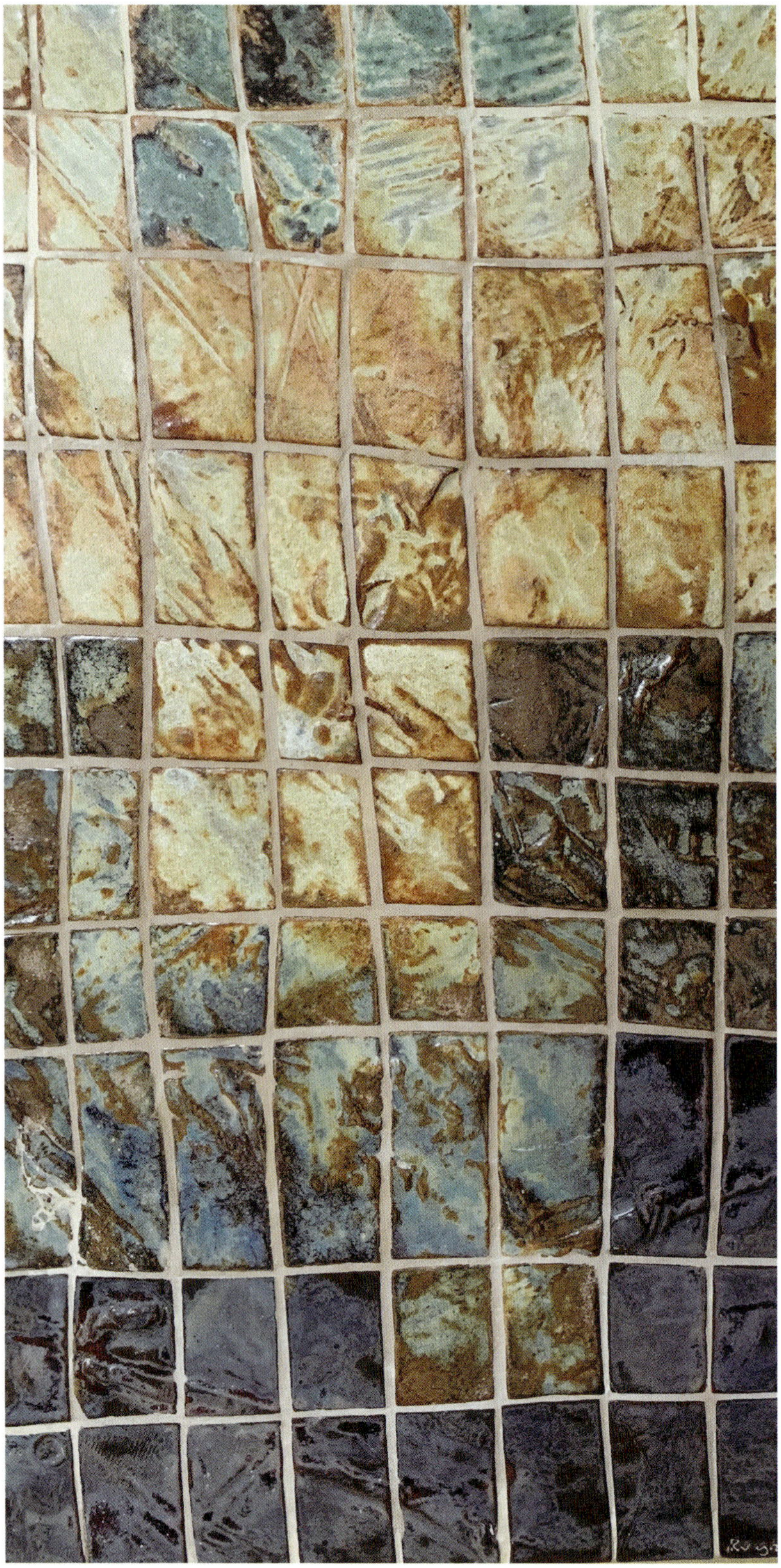

Earth section maquette for a meditative nave at the Washington National Cathedral; 24" × 44" (61cm × 112cm)

THE RIGHT QUESTION

Not long after my escapade with the paint and the shower, I realized I needed to learn a bit more about painting techniques and started lessons with another artist. Over and over again, she would ask, "Do you like it?"

I wanted to know if it was "good." But the more important questions are, "Do you like it? Does it make your heart sing? Does it match your inner vision? Is it you?" When I realized I could do whatever I wanted to do, it was a lightbulb moment. I could have fun. I could do what I liked. I could play. The freedom of it made me giddy.

The process reminded me of a retrospective of Alexander Calder's work I saw in my early twenties, when I was working as a bank examiner. I wandered through the show, which featured Calder's innovative, playful hanging mobiles and wire sculptures, and my disciplined, structured self was a little shocked. "He's just having fun," I thought.

Now, of course, I know making art is more than just fun. It is an exploration. It is finding that inner voice that wants to be heard. It's listening, watching, paying attention. It's letting the divine come through our grounded selves.

I have come to think making art is about learning to trust our own inner voice and to stay with that vision even when it might be considered out-of-sync with current tastes. Who knows? Perhaps making art is the universe's way of teaching self-confidence and self-esteem?

CHANGING MEDIUMS

Fast forward to 2014. By then I had been working with clay for more than thirty years (while continuing my consulting career). I knew glazes and clay bodies and firing processes. I knew what I needed to do to achieve the effects I wanted. However, a restlessness surged yet again.

This time, I fought change.

For years, I loved the feeling of holding clay; it's both alive and calming. I loved the way I could manipulate it to get texture in a piece. I loved the excitement of opening the kiln and seeing how the magic of heat had changed the work inside.

But I tired of the dust and the glaze and the chemicals, so I sold all my ceramic supplies and kilns to a couple setting up their own clay studio. I was saying goodbye to a big chunk of my life.

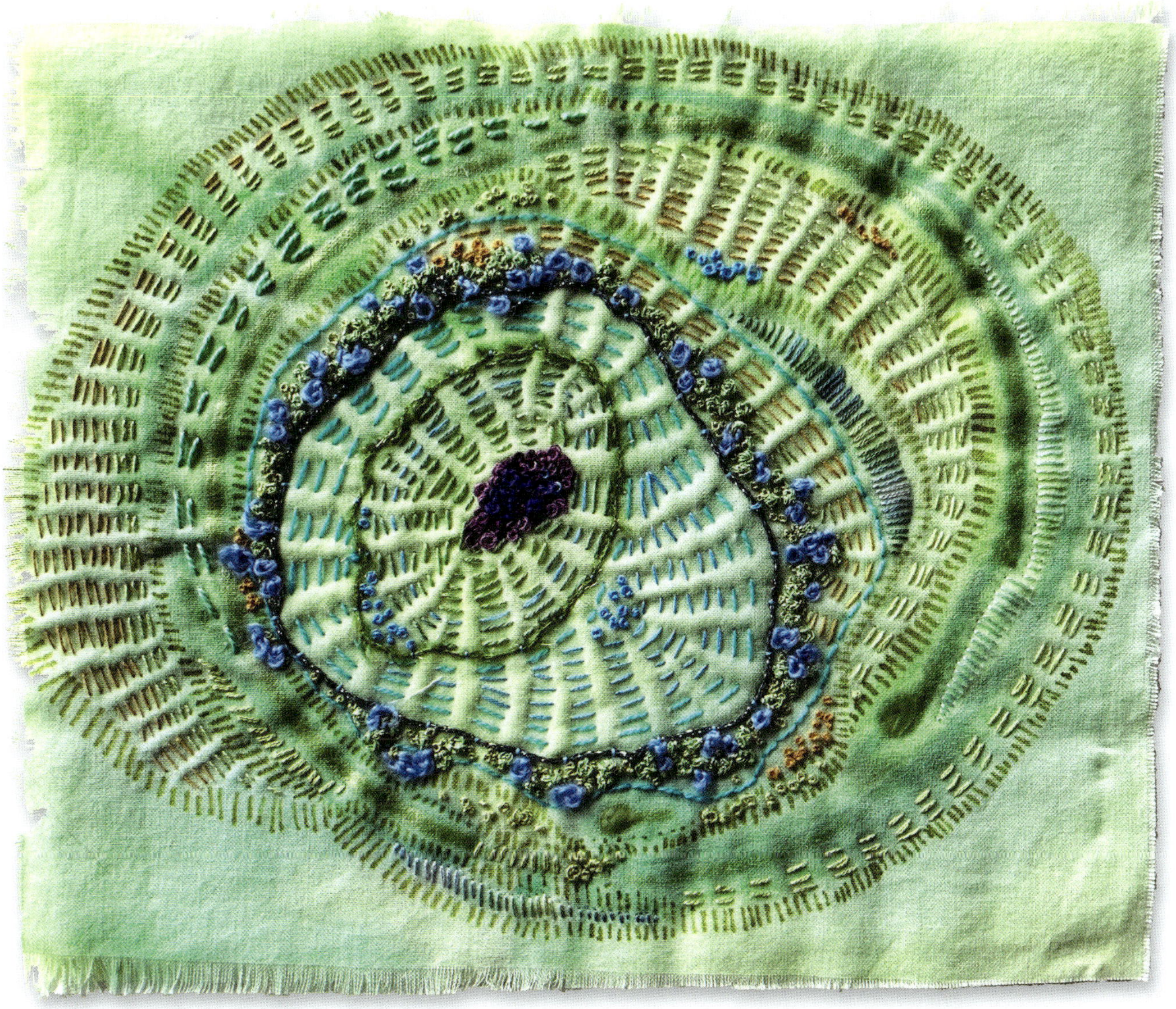

Amoeba
Learning a new medium. Stitch on hand-dyed cotton; 8" × 8" (20cm × 20cm)

Just as clay had grabbed me and filled my dreams and reveries so long ago, the work of textile artists—soft yarns, hand-dyed fabric, silk threads, and gorgeous color—began to entice me in the same way. It was like falling in love again: exciting, demanding, and unrelenting.

I started by piecing some fabric together. Ooh, I liked it. I took classes on machine and hand stitching. I built a studio library on hand-dyeing and started the process of learning a new medium. I tried felting and collage and made some labor-intensive, large pieces of stitch work—all part of an exploration process—trying to find how to make the pieces that would feel like magic to me.

Change can be so hard. And renewing. And necessary.

My curiosity was alive. Joy came back into my new studio.

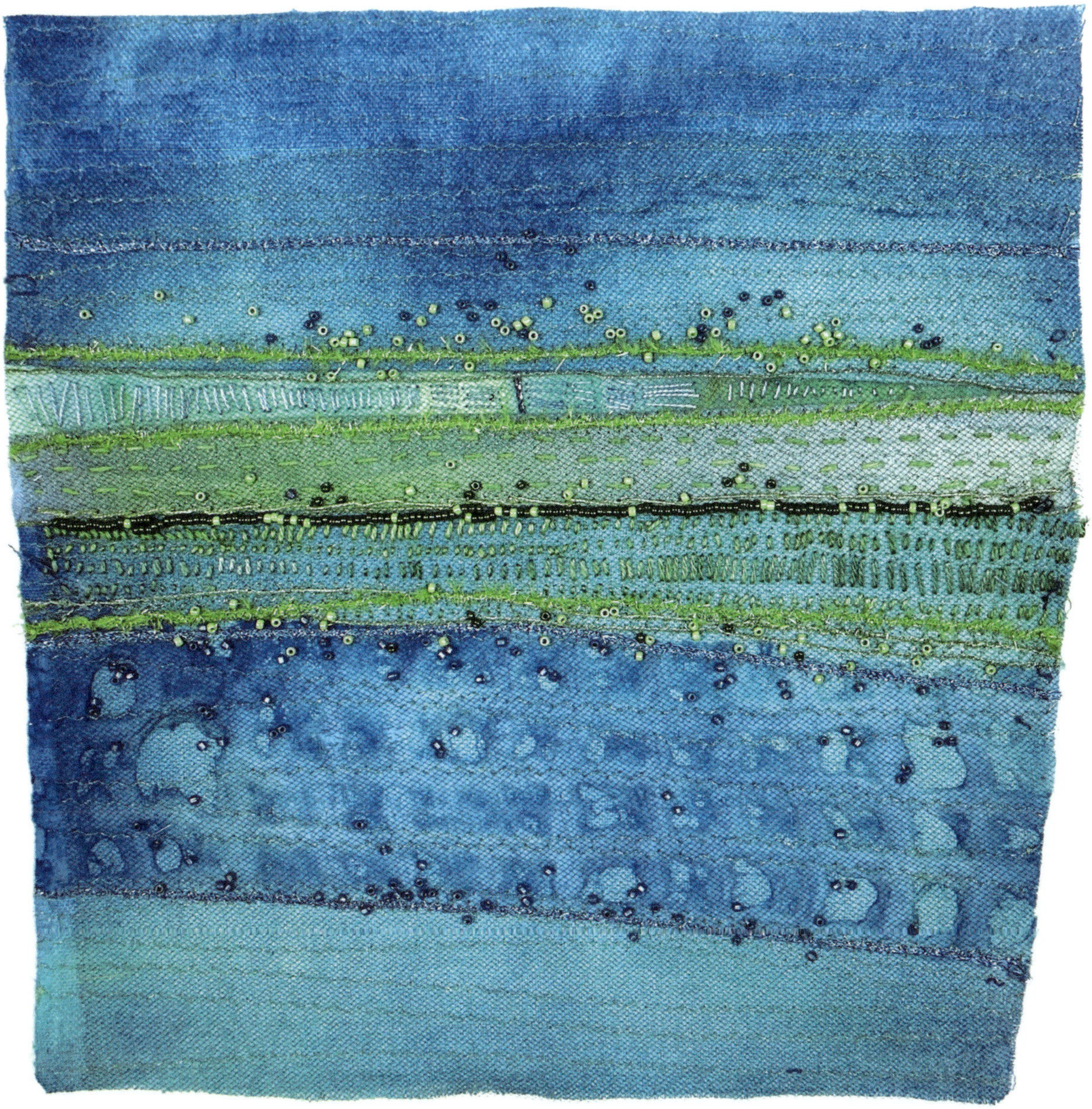

Blue Fields
Learning a new medium. Hand-dyed linen, rice paper, and tulle with lots of stitch and beads; 8″ × 8″ (20cm × 20cm)

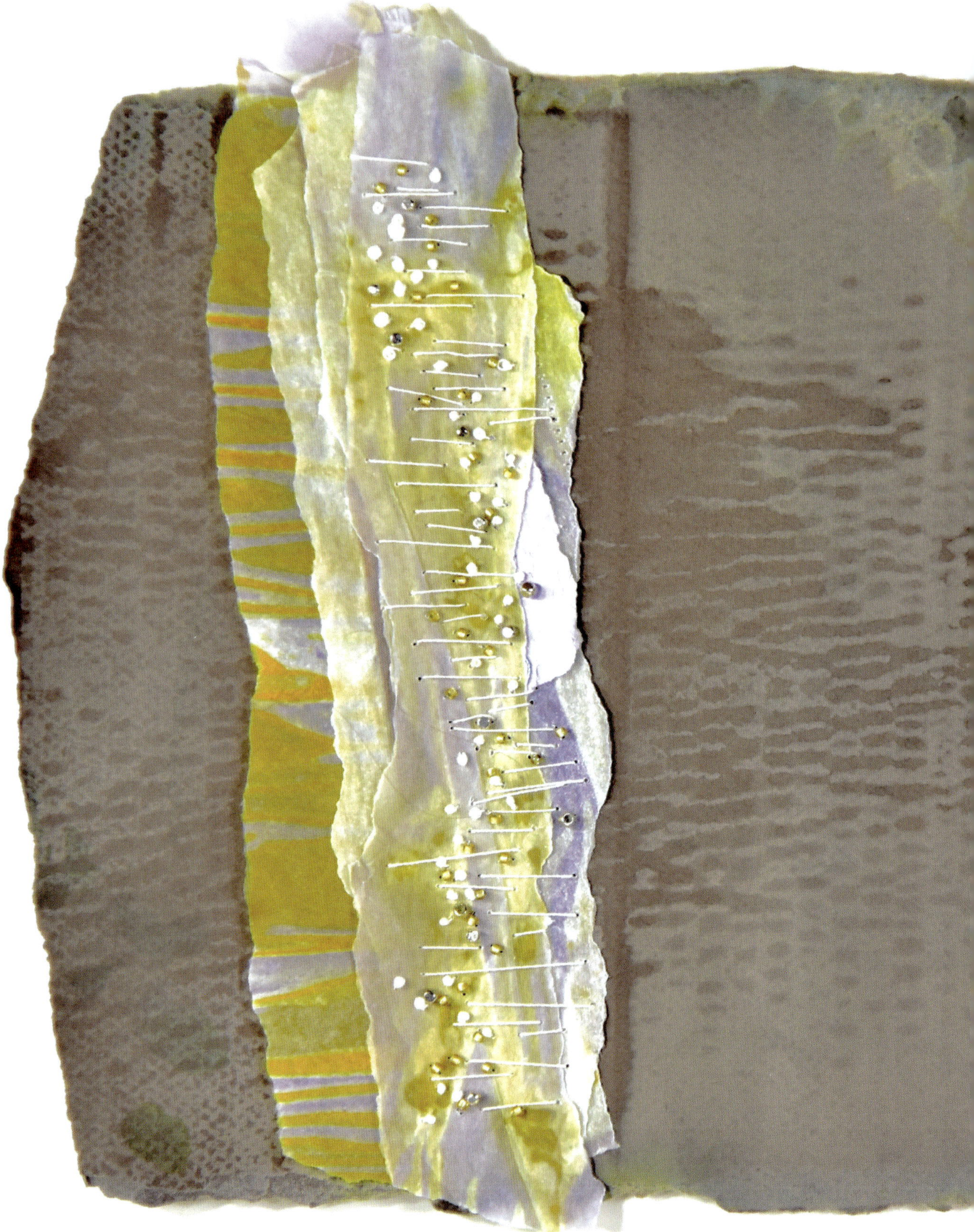

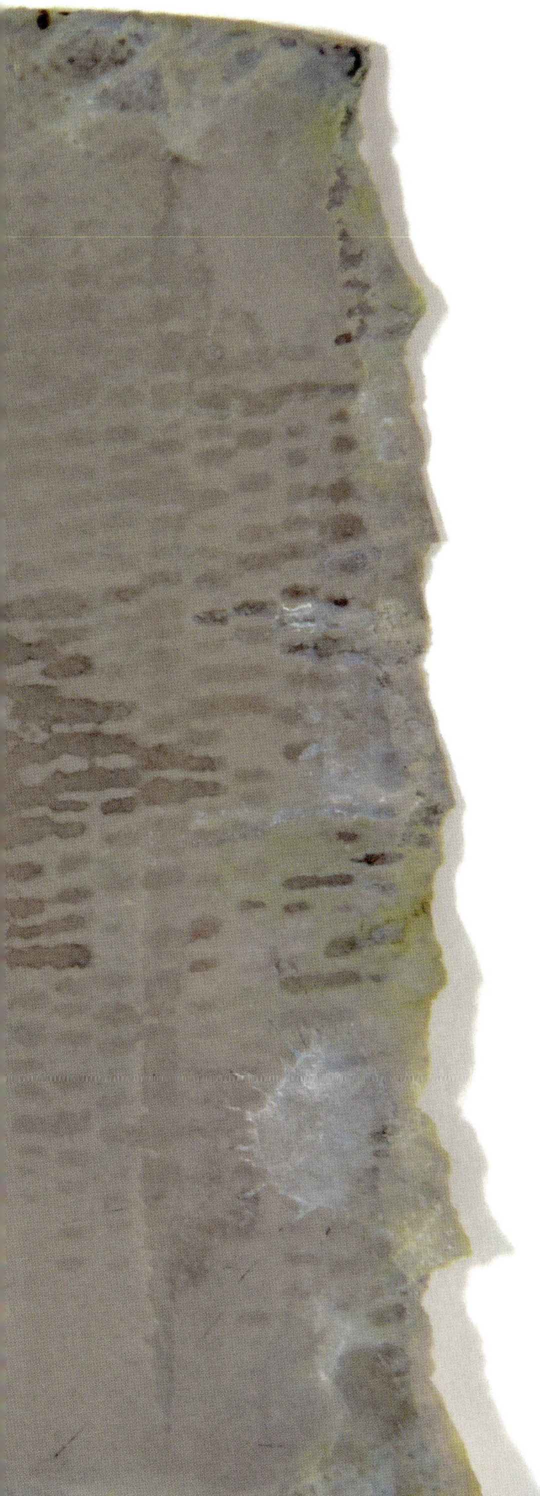

THE INFILL

Small Art • Sparkle • Fields • Clouds • The Long View • Wabi-Sabi • Movement • In Person • Other Artists • Serendipity and Synchronicity • Close-Ups • Abstract Art • Tree Bark • Fields Again • Love • Granpi's Garden • Past Work • Ethereal • Fragments • Parallel • A Long Life • Letting Go • Retrospectives • The In-Between • Moving On • Frustration • Evolution • Movement Again • Flow • Time • The Divine • Discipline • Inner and Outer Worlds • Makers • Patience • Ground Covers • Pause • Stardust

Tidelands Series
Botanically-dyed papers and stitch; 10″ × 9″ (25cm ×23cm)

SMALL ART

My love affair with small pieces of art had begun on that first day when I cut up my big pieces of "ruined" paper to find the little jewels within. Now, whenever I start feeling "stuck" in the studio, I go back to making small pieces.

I love the intimacy of a small piece. It pulls me in and gets me looking at the details. It's like I become Alice in Wonderland, shrinking myself inside the piece, another world where I can live for a moment or two. They're more feminine. They permit a quick gesture, a focused thought, a small detail.

Larger pieces are bold and demanding, and sometimes that is magical, too. But smaller pieces creep up on us and ask us to pay attention to the detail.

When I first started cutting up my larger pieces, I made so many little pieces that I began to make art cards, and at different times, I've sold some of them. Constance Kay in New York has a wonderful hand-made art-card business called A Little Piece of Art, and I made cards for her for a while. I also sold many myself, and I gave a lot of them away. I loved the idea of hundreds of little pieces of art sailing out into the world.

Even now, when I can sometimes successfully make large pieces, I love to take the corner of a larger piece and, in my mind's eye, turn it into a smaller piece. In fact, I have gone so far as to cut up many of my larger pieces to create smaller ones because they have charming details that are often lost in the bigger piece.

Lately, I have been making cards again. They tickle me. But then I get to thinking, "I should make some bigger pieces." Sometimes those "shoulds" really get in our way.

For today, I am relishing making small pieces.

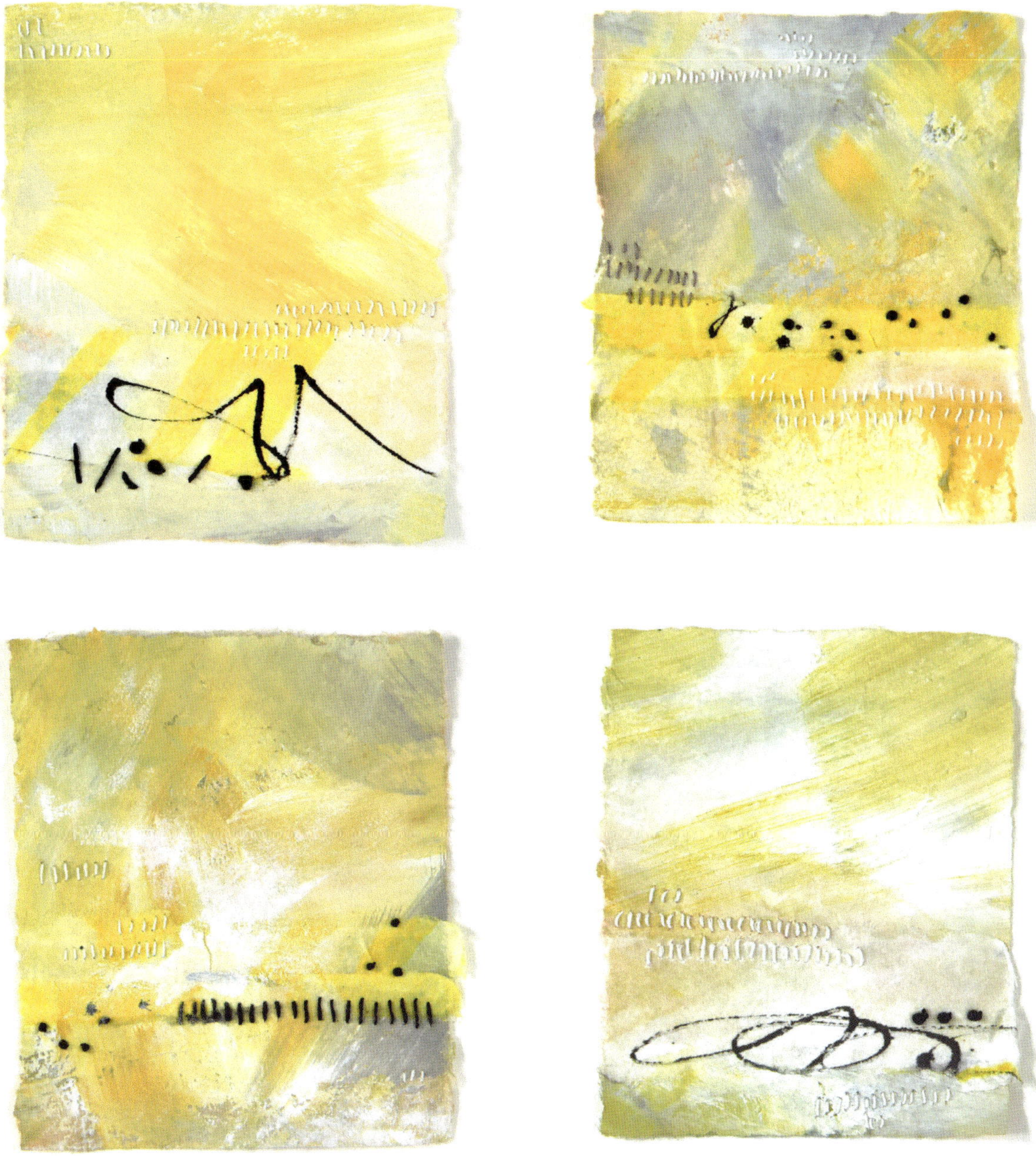

Enigma
Washi paper collage with stitch, part of a 12-piece series, 4" x 5" (10cm x 13cm)

SPARKLE

When I was young, before car seats and safety laws, I loved to curl up in the back window of my family's sedan as we drove through the Minnesota countryside from Saint Paul to Fairfax on the way to visit my dad's parents. From that perch, I could look up at the twinkling stars and be away from my crowding sisters. It's farm country there; few trees block the sky and few lights dim the stars. On cloudless nights, the night sky would come alive, and I would get lost in it.

The night sky has been there to encourage me at several pivotal times in my life. There was a time when I was living in Topanga, California, in the Santa Monica Mountains and unsure of my next step. I would look up at the night sky and, in an intuitive flash, know that I was the only me on the planet. I knew in that moment that we each need to bring our full selves to life because we cannot be replaced.

Glistening light on snow. Sunlight hitting water. Leaves lit up with raindrops. All of these remind me of the night sky and my connection to something larger than myself.

Now, I like to add a bit of sparkle to my artwork; I can't help it. Opalescent inks, shiny threads, a few glossy beads. I try not to overdo it, but, like crows, I love a little bit of sparkle.

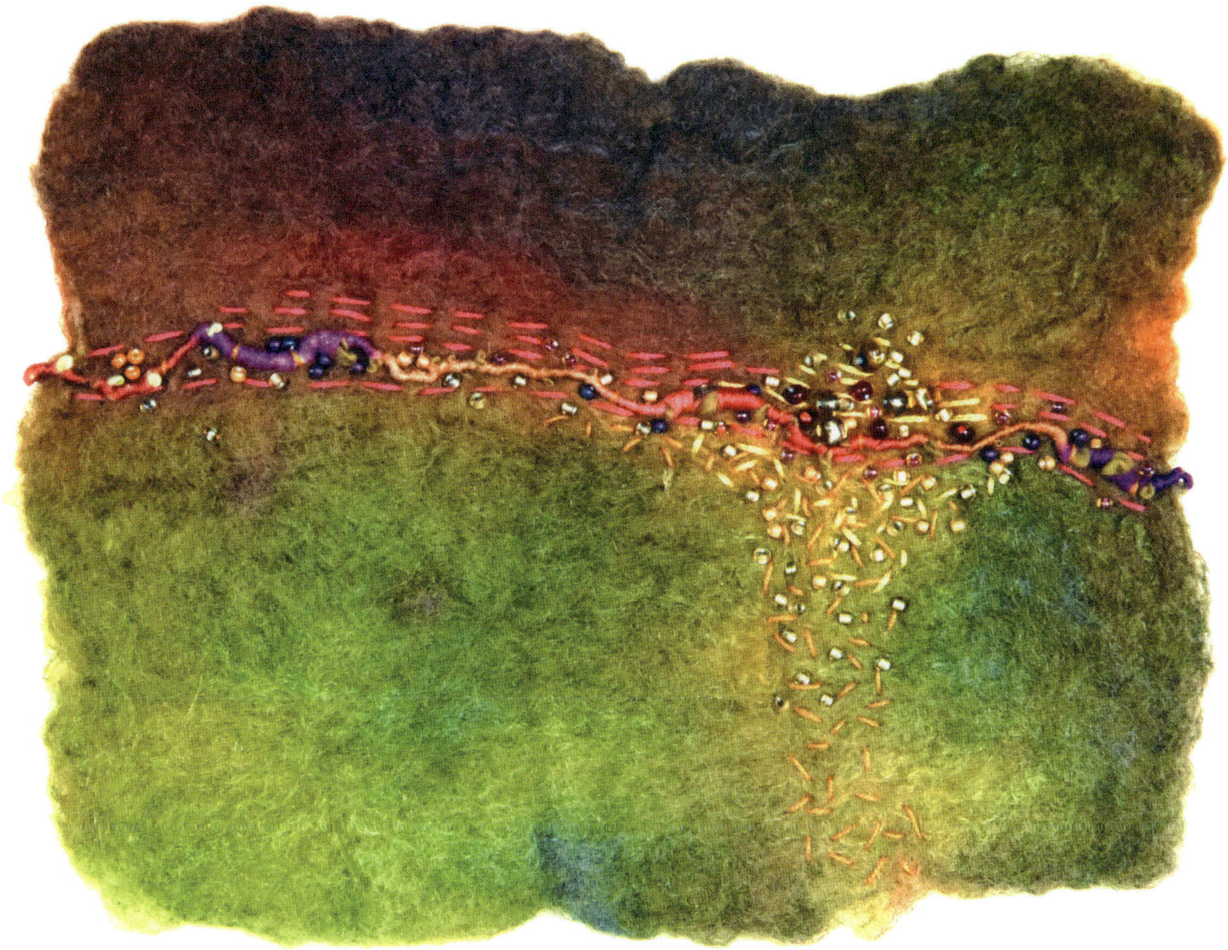

Sunrise
Hand-dyed felt and stitch; 6″ × 5″ (15cm ×13cm)

FIELDS

Some Native Americans say it takes seven generations to get used to "new ground" and to feel like you've sprung from that ground. That may be true. I "sprung up" from Minnesota ground, and her cornfields must be buried deep in my psyche as the patterns of fields so often seep into my work.

I love the window seat on an airplane so I can look at patterns on the Earth below. Now Google Earth makes virtual "window seats" available all the time and all over the world. I have spent hours trolling over those maps looking at fields around the world. Not all fields are as square and straight as the Minnesota and North Dakota fields; many wander asymmetrically around the contours of the land. I like that, but I most often stitch the square, repetitive patterns of my home ground.

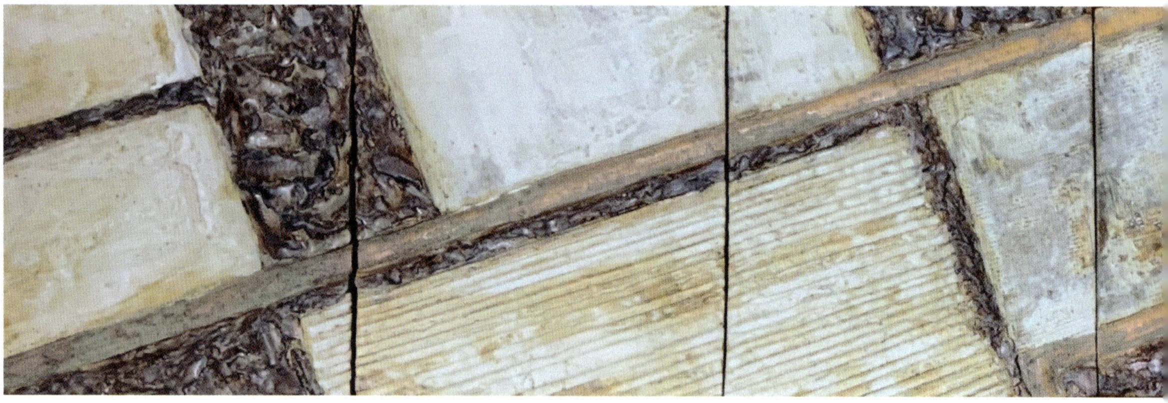

The monocultures of Minnesota and North Dakota fields are contrary to my own beliefs about the best ways to garden and let nature thrive. Yet, those fields are still in me. I love the industriousness that's required to make them. I love the patterns they form and the colors as the seasons change.

My first field pieces were done in memory of my dad; a series of ceramic pieces for a show I was having in Virginia.

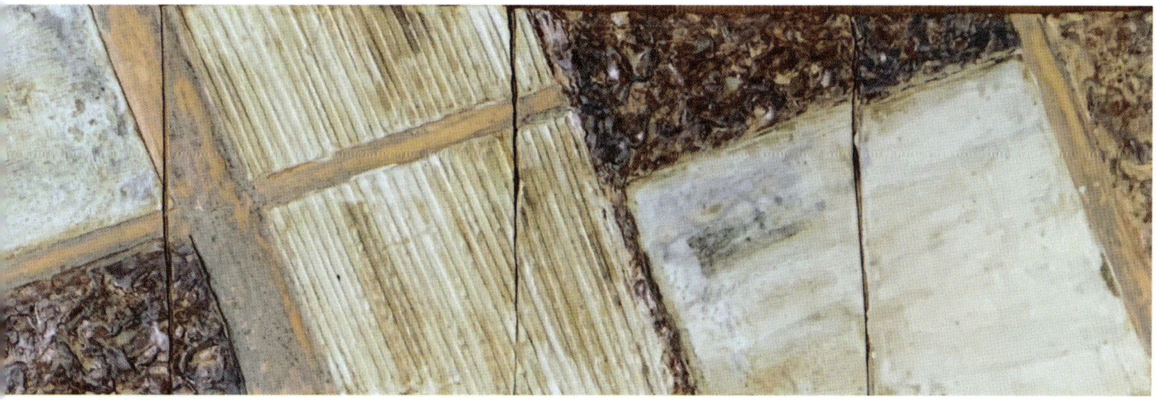

North Dakota Fields
Stoneware with multiple glazes. Each tile - 12" × 13" (31cm × 33cm); entire piece - 84" × 13" (213cm × 33cm)

Here's what I wrote about them then:

> *"My father, John F. Wagner, died on September 1, 2000. During the past year, I've thought about the wisdom he gained during his lifetime and have come to believe that a good part of it was attributable to the North Dakota landscape. He loved to drive those roads and was usually able to find work that permitted it. The endless long views, the moving fields, the big sky, and the quiet rhythms encouraged—I believe—a form of moving meditation that allowed a deeply quiet wisdom to emerge. These pieces are a tribute to him and that landscape. In making them, I found that the openness and simplicity of the landscape demanded a new quiet in me, as well."*

CLOUDS

Recently, I flew to San Francisco because of my consulting work. The cumulus clouds seen from above were magnificent, frothy balls that felt like they would surely be the best trampoline in the world. I remember the first time I saw them. In our teens, my sister Kate and I flew to Los Angeles to visit our aunt and uncle. What a gift we have been given to have that perspective of Earth.

When I first started painting with water media, the paint would pool in cloud-like bundles, and I was happy to just leave it at that. As I learned more, I thought, "That's not enough. I need to make it more like a 'real' painting."

After that trip to San Francisco, though, I thought maybe I would leave fields alone for a bit and go back to clouds. And be content with the way paint pools.

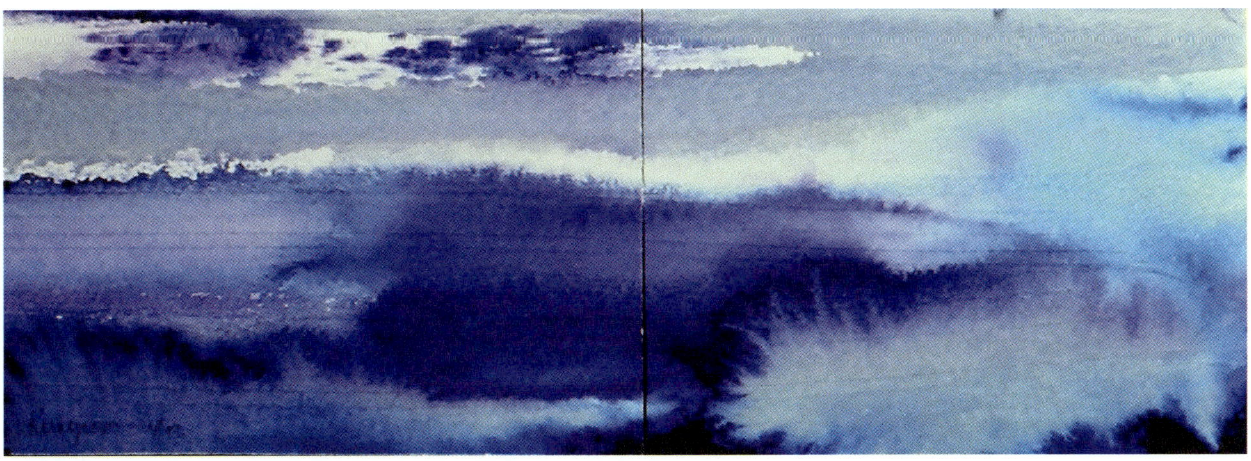

Clouds
Water media on Arches paper, 13.5" × 5" (34cm × 13cm)

THE LONG VIEW

I remember driving around North Dakota with my dad and his glee over being able to see a stand of trees that he knew was sixty miles away. The horizon line in the Dakotas is ever-present.

It must be in my genes; no matter what is happening in the close-up of my life, even a brief glimpse at the horizon will take me out of myself and remind me of the bigger picture.

Nowadays I have a view of Washington's Puget Sound and a huge slice of sky. My house sits high on a hill, and I love having that expansive view of the water and sky. When I am not obsessing on fields or clouds, the horizon line will call.

A few years ago, during a tough time in the non-art portion of my life, I decided to make a small horizon line piece each morning for a month to remind me to look up. It brought a bit of joy to every day, and at the end of the month, I had a collection of pieces that I loved.

I am looking toward eternity in them.

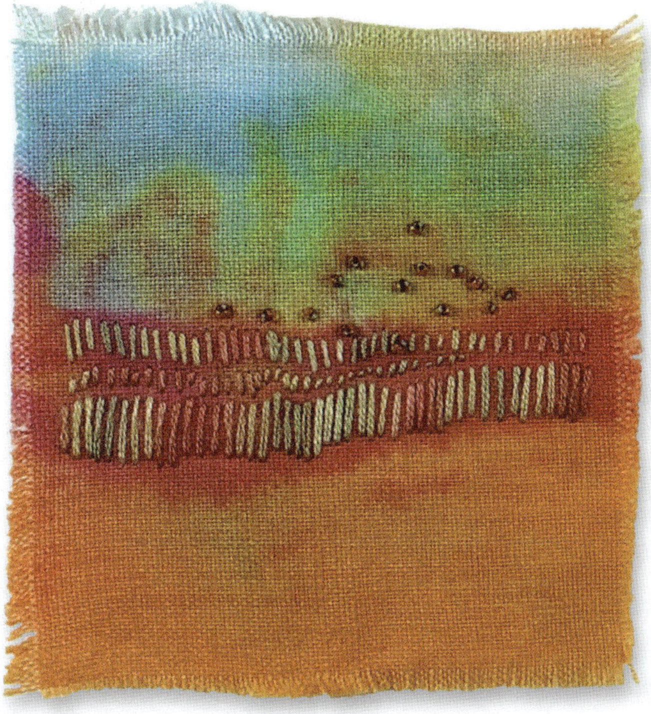

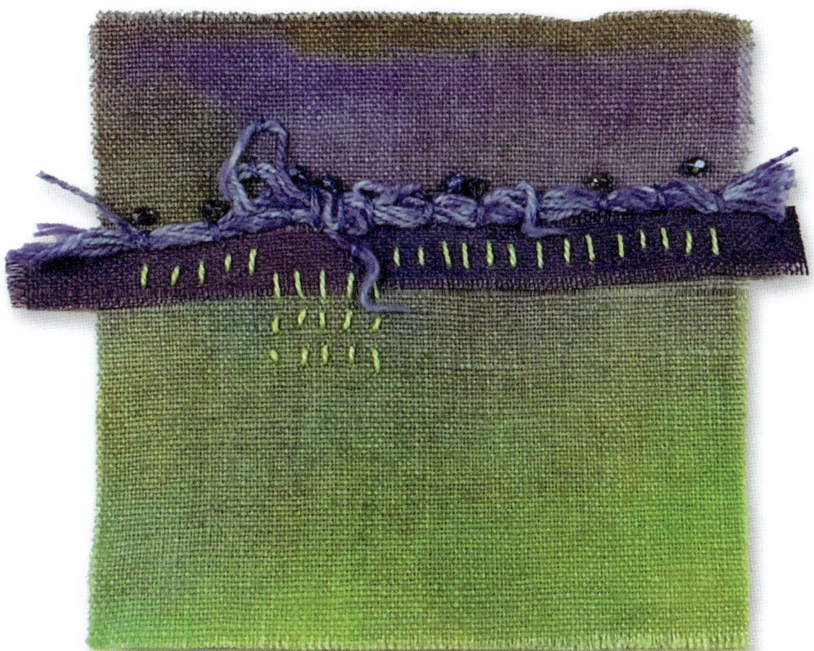

These pieces are part of a series. The pieces are tiny–4" × 4" (10cm × 10cm)–and made with hand-dyed fabric, papers or felt. By keeping them small, I could make one each day.

WABI-SABI

Wabi-sabi is a Japanese concept with layers and layers of meaning so, of course, I love it. Many books have been written on it, and lately it seems that everyone is talking about it. For me, it juxtaposes new life with signs of decay to remind us to embrace all of life in the moment.

Early one spring, a foxglove was growing in a decaying retaining wall on our property. I loved seeing something new that was born on something old. They looked beautiful together. I've been impatient to replace that old decaying wall, but, seeing the foxglove, I knew the new wall would come soon enough.

I like the juxtaposition of new and old in artwork, too. It's why I like the frayed edges of fabric on my pieces. I don't want it to look too perfect.

Wabi-sabi took on a new meaning for me when Bruce was diagnosed with Parkinson's disease. His increasing frailty and age reminded me to cherish every moment, not just those shiny new moments. I respect the path that has brought him to this point in his life with all the combinations of memories and new births that have been part of it.

We tend to want to blot out old age and the frailty it brings. It makes us uncomfortable. But for me, these months remind me how precious life is with all the memories and dreams that are born and die during a lifetime. It reminds me to be where I am right now, because this moment will never come again.

I hope a little bit of that comes through in my artwork.

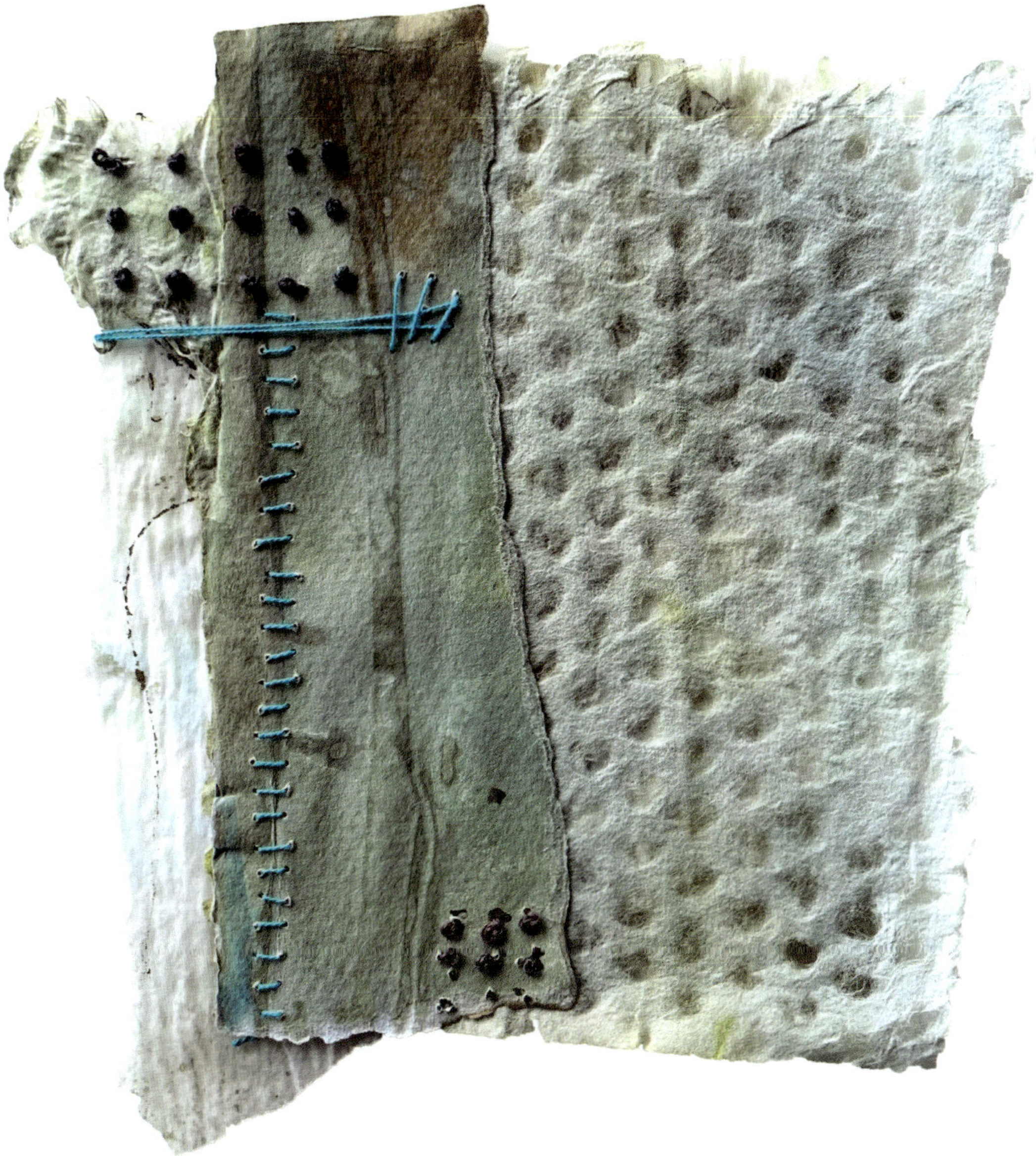

Sea Wall
Collage with stitch and botanically-dyed rice, parchment and art paper;
6" × 6" (15cm ×15cm)

MOVEMENT

I love the feel of movement in artwork; think of the (Robert) Motherwell swoosh of black paint. It's one of the things I miss about painting. With one arm gesture and a brush loaded with paint I could create the feeling of movement.

Another fine example of this is the Maurice Prendergast *Umbrellas in the Rain* painting. He was a master at moving our eyes from one splotch of red to the next.

With fabrics and stitch, more often than not, I need to use the Prendergast approach to movement. The process of moving hands and eyes in stitch becomes the meditation.

I miss that larger movement, though, and hope I'll find a way to incorporate that in my artwork again someday.

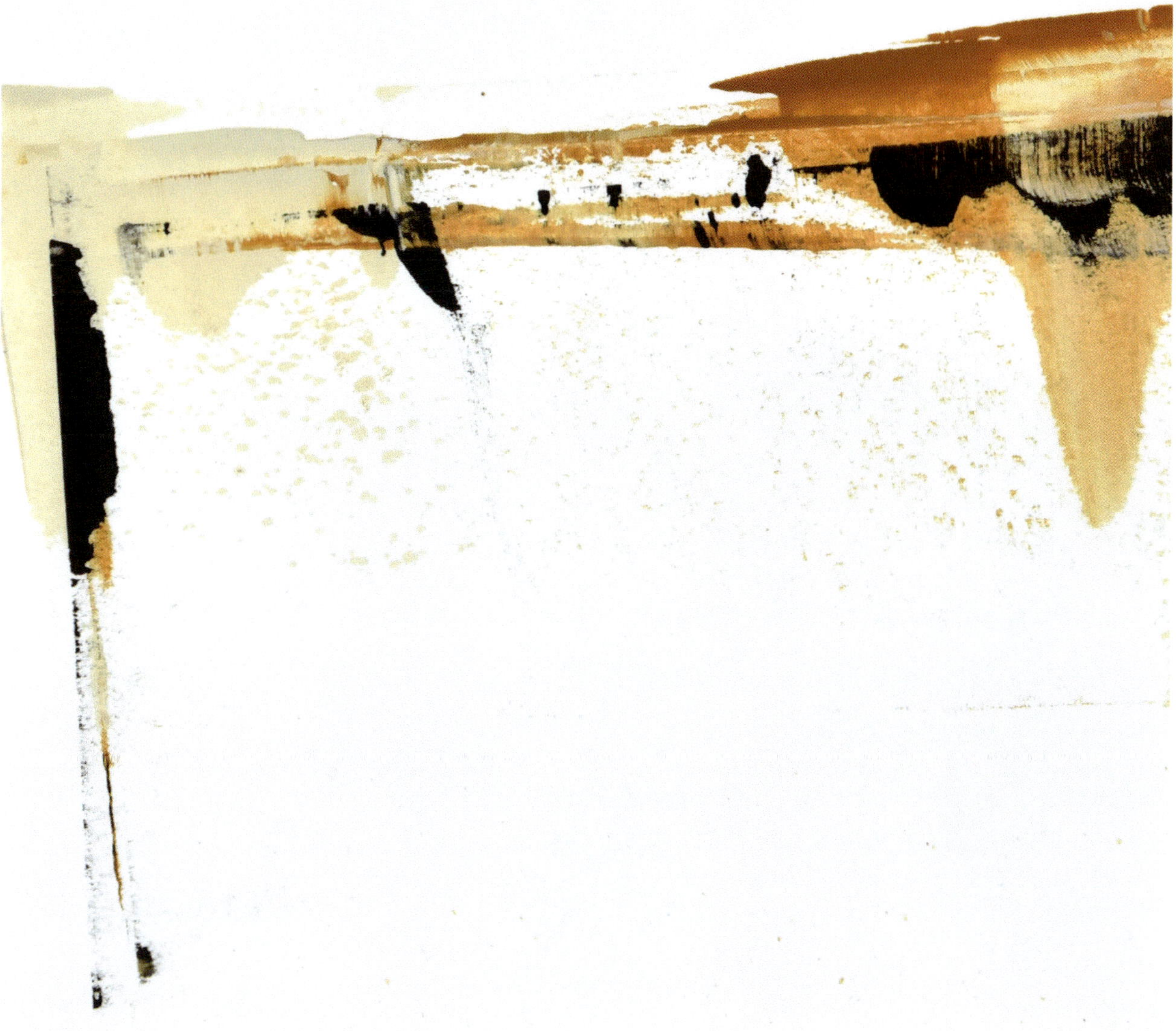

Journal page, 6" x 6" (15cm x 15cm(

IN PERSON

Pinterest and Instagram give us access to the work of artists that would have been impossible for us to see so easily even a decade ago. It's a privilege to be able to look at so much art so easily.

However, it is not the same as seeing a piece in person. Dr. Barnes, for example, did not allow his great paintings to be photographed during his lifetime, because he knew they were not the same in a photograph.

The color is never exactly right in a photograph. The brushstrokes and the textures don't come through the same way. And there is that little bit of magic that comes from the artist's touch; the imprint they leave in their work that can't be captured in a photograph. It's as if we get a sense of the great masters themselves when we see a piece of their work in person.

So . . . go to museums, go to galleries, and see as much as you can firsthand. Buy original art that you love—hopefully from a local artist. It will change the way your home feels, and you'll help an artist continue with his or her work.

I, too, need to be reminded of this again and again. I recently stopped into a local gallery and saw the work of Sharon Carr, a Gig Harbor, Washington artist. Wow! The texture with encaustic was magical.

OTHER ARTISTS

The best artists' works stop me in my tracks. It's a state beyond words, akin to a mystical experience. Time stops.

Rennie Mackintosh, Helen Frankenthaler, Rothko, Motherwell, of course Van Gogh, and many other artists have touched me that way. Most recently, Debbie Lyddon, Helen Terry, and Shelley Rhodes— all textile artists in the United Kingdom—have stunned me with their work. I live in the world of their vision for a while.

The best artists forever change the way I see their subject matter. A copse will never be the same after seeing Wolf Kahn's tree paintings. Once I saw a blueberry bush that had a smattering of bright yellow and orange leaves still hanging from its limbs, and Rick Stevens's paintings popped into my mind. They often include splotches of yellow and gold that seem to hang in the air, like bits of a divine light.

As much as I have loved opening the door to the larger world, it's also good to find our own tribe, one we are in-sync with. For me, Instagram and Pinterest have opened a whole new world of like-minded souls. Other artists are my tribe.

SERENDIPITY AND SYNCHRONICITY

My garden has many plants that self-seed. I love foxgloves, columbines, and Welsh poppies. They can be quite invasive, especially the poppies. I have been warned to get them out of the garden, and perhaps someday I will wish that I had. But in the spring, I love seeing where they set themselves. They come up in the most charming of spots and give splashes of yellow and orange. I spread their seeds in parts of the garden where they have never been before and hope I don't regret that someday. But I can see them weaving themselves through the garden, helping to make it a unified space.

I like that kind of randomness in the studio, too. I like some splashes of paint to land wherever they want. I like the way glazes in a kiln will sometimes do magical things. I like it when I never know for sure what will happen. Sometimes I like the result, and sometimes it's a disaster. But when it works, it's magical and something I could never recreate if I tried.

The serendipity of a foxglove landing in exactly the right spot, paint blending in the most magical way, or a ceramic glaze pooling in exactly the right crevice never fails to delight and surprise me.

I love the precise detail evident in some of the great painted manuscripts or the work of great illustrators. I admire the control needed to accomplish it and think of the quiet, meditative work it requires. But for me, serendipity—the happy mistake—takes the piece beyond me and allows the universe to help me make it.

I like that.

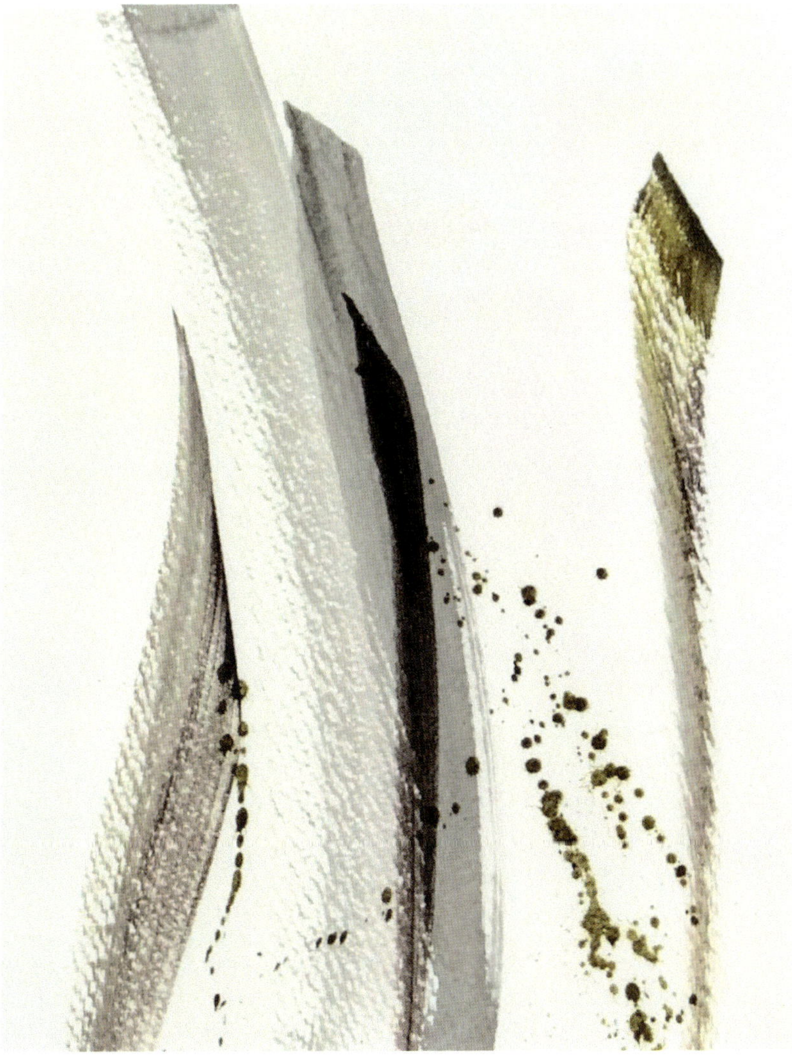

Synchronicity
Water media on cotton paper, 9" × 12" (23cm ×30cm)

CLOSE-UPS

Almost three decades ago, on my drive to upstate New York for Jean Houston's Mystery School, intuition pulled me off onto a country road. At a used bookstore out there in the middle of nowhere I found a book called *Interior World of Gemstones* by E. Gübelin. It is filled with photographs of gemstones under high magnification.

That book has inspired me ever since.

So many of his photos remind me of the pictures we see from the Hubble Space Telescope. It's a wonder that the high magnification of a microscope can also look like deep space.

I love when artwork captures an image that could come from a microscope or a telescope. It reminds me that the finite and the infinite are connected and of the same matter.

Otto Natzler's glazes, and the photographs of them, all have that surreal outer space or high magnification feel to them. Vally's glazes had that, too. Here is one of mine.

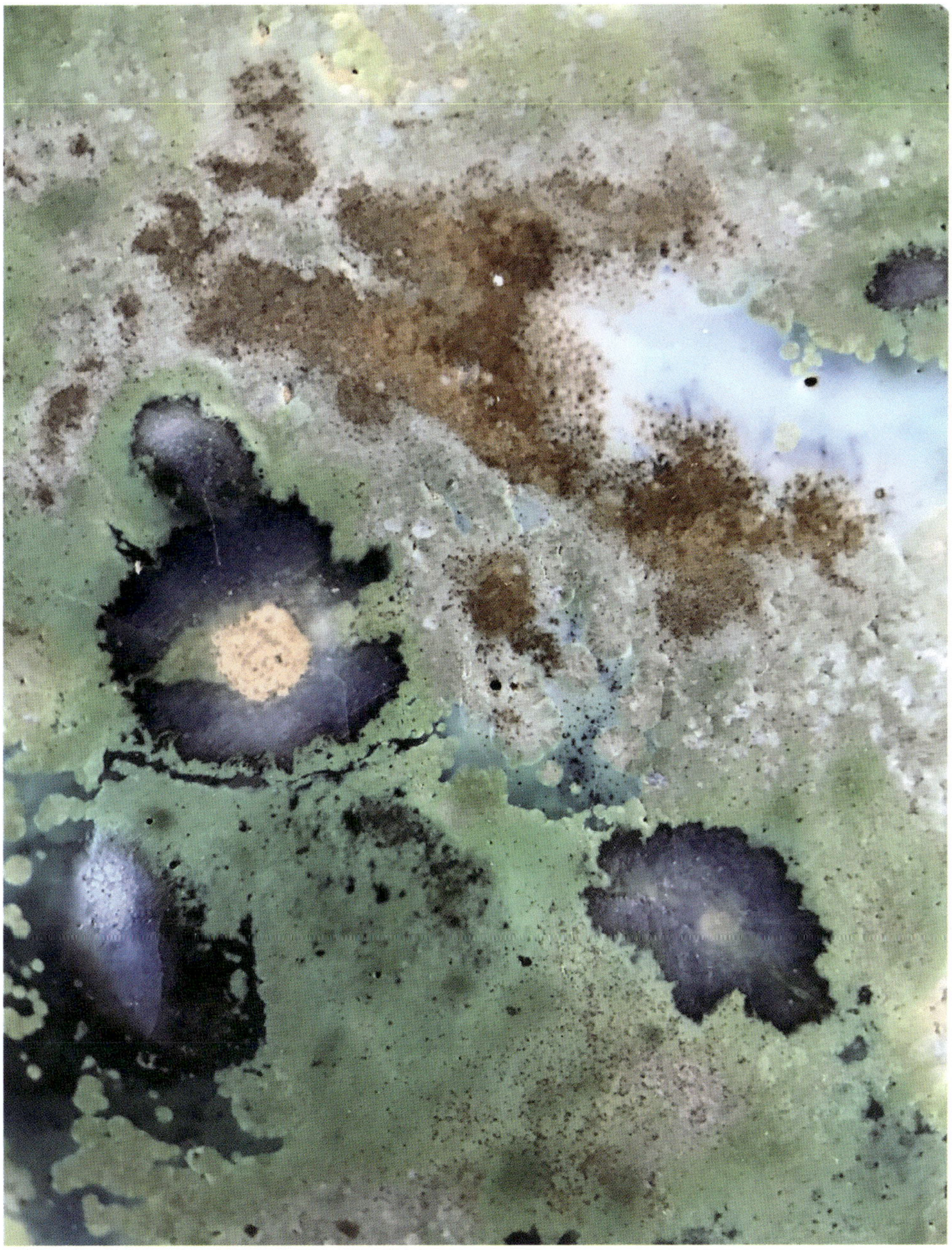

Close-up photo of my ceramic glazes with a transferred value of Earth from space or a view from under a microscope.

ABSTRACT ART

Mid-20th century sculptor Anne Truitt writes beautifully about the influence of being born with undiagnosed nearsightedness and its influence on her view of the world and art. She speculates that it is partially why she is attracted to abstract art.

I'm badly nearsighted, too. Without my glasses, the world will often look like a Rothko painting. As a result, undefined and blurry landscapes are comfortable; I recognize them.

Dr. Barnes did not appreciate abstract art because he felt the image being painted should reinforce the "plastic quality," as he called it, of the paint itself. By "plastic quality" he meant the texture and feel of the brushstroke. Little wispy brushstrokes would lend themselves to a painting that had a transferred value of delicacy or fragility, while strong brushstrokes and thick paint might have a transferred value of strength and power. Think of some of Cézanne's seated figures. The perspective is often from knee-level looking up at the strong figure and the brushstrokes support this impression.

But I was drawn to abstract art because it feels universal to me. An abstracted landscape could be the plains of North Dakota or a sweep of Puget Sound. It might remind me of Minnesota lakes, and someone else of Cape Cod.

When done well, I let the color, the movement, and the paint of an abstracted piece surround me. As time stops, I "enter" the painting. Helen Frankenthaler was one of the first artists whose work touched me that way. Decades ago, I went to see a retrospective of hers and let myself wander among her paintings. One painting after another. They are magic if you don't try to figure them out. No specific place or person pulls your thoughts into some earthbound story.

We can be in the universe for a moment.

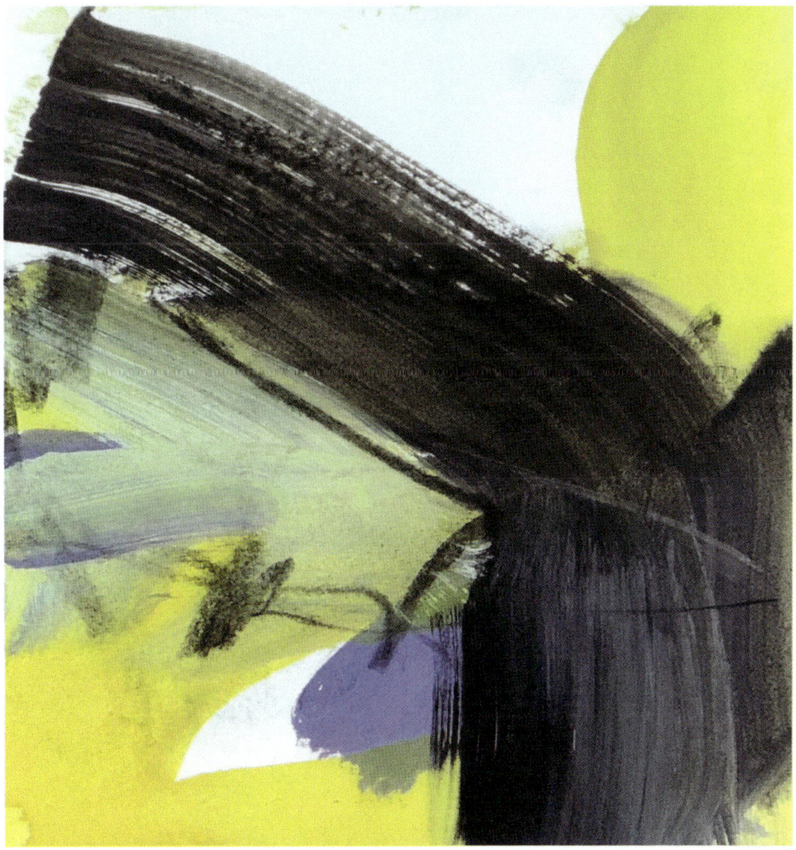

Journal page, 8" × 8" (20cm × 20cm)

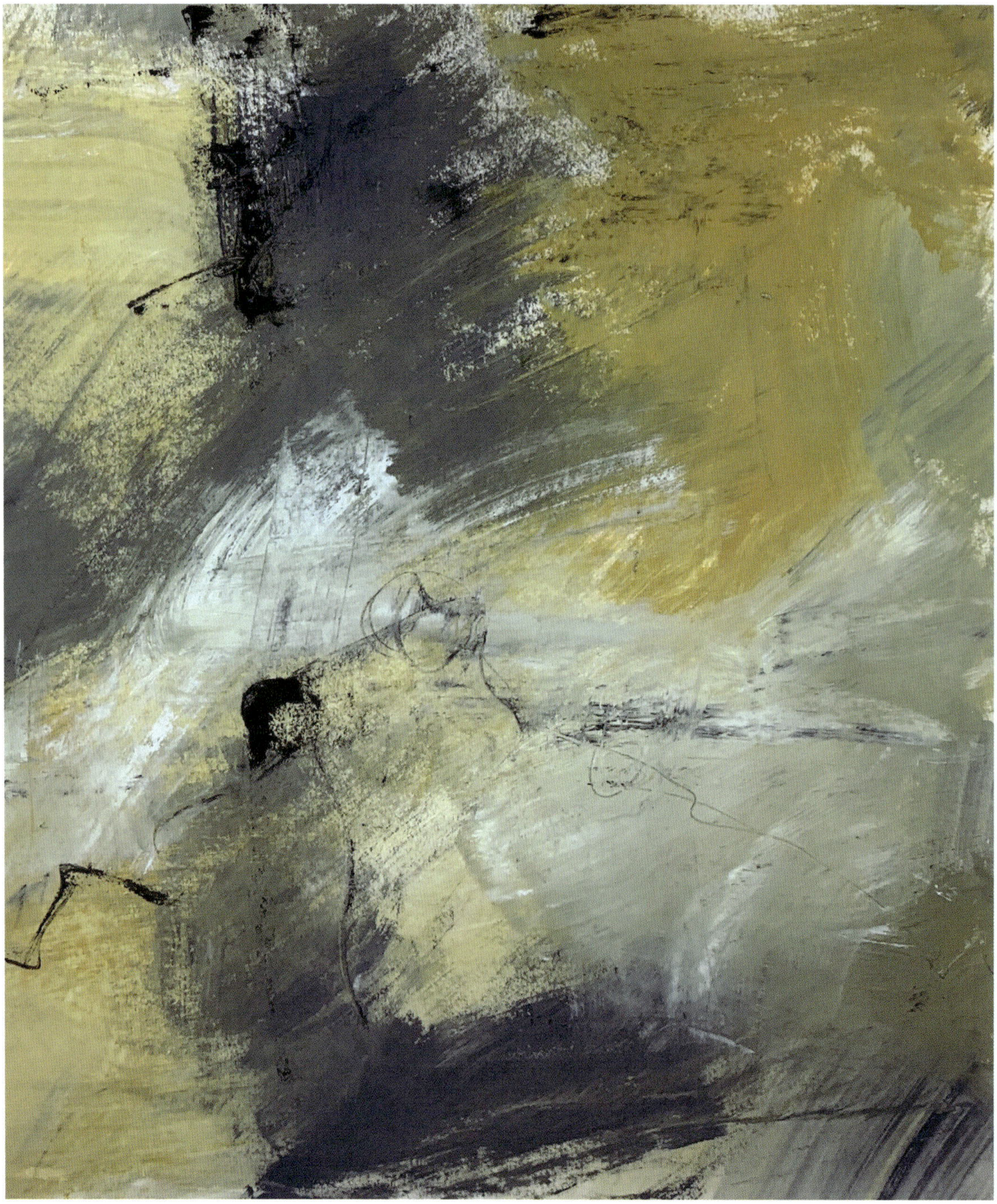

Pacific Northwest; Diptych
Acrylic and India ink on washi paper, each 20" × 24" (51cm × 61cm)

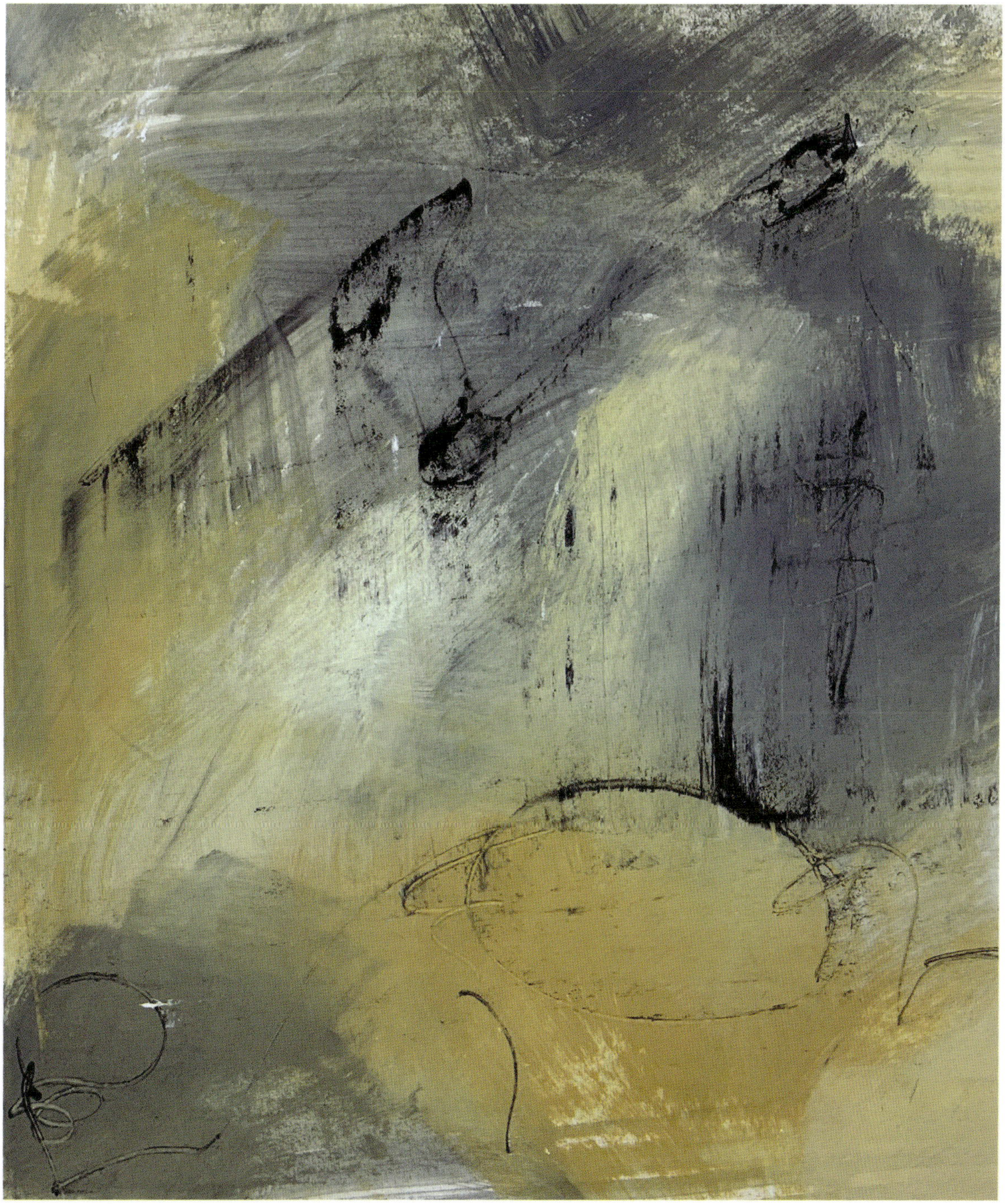

TREE BARK

I have always loved trees and have sometimes crammed too many in a garden. When we lived in Virginia and had eleven acres, I dreamed of planting a birch tree copse in a field. I imagined hundreds of trees. I never got the chance to do that. Sometimes we are saved from ourselves.

Bruce was doing physical therapy for his Parkinson's at our local hospital, which has a magical wellness garden that includes a slew of birch trees. Floor-to-ceiling windows in the therapy room look out on the garden, and my attention often wandered to those trees and their beautiful bark.

Subsequently, I started making birch bark pieces. I stitch parchment paper that was used in botanical printmaking into folded, bark-like segments and add bits of botanically-dyed silk, rice paper, and wool to the mix. I love these little pieces.

On my daily walk, I look more carefully at the trees. Wow! There's a whole world of bark to capture. Living in the Pacific Northwest, many of our trees have mosses and lichens growing on their bark. Imagine that in thread.

I guess I can leave fields and clouds for a while and think about tree bark.

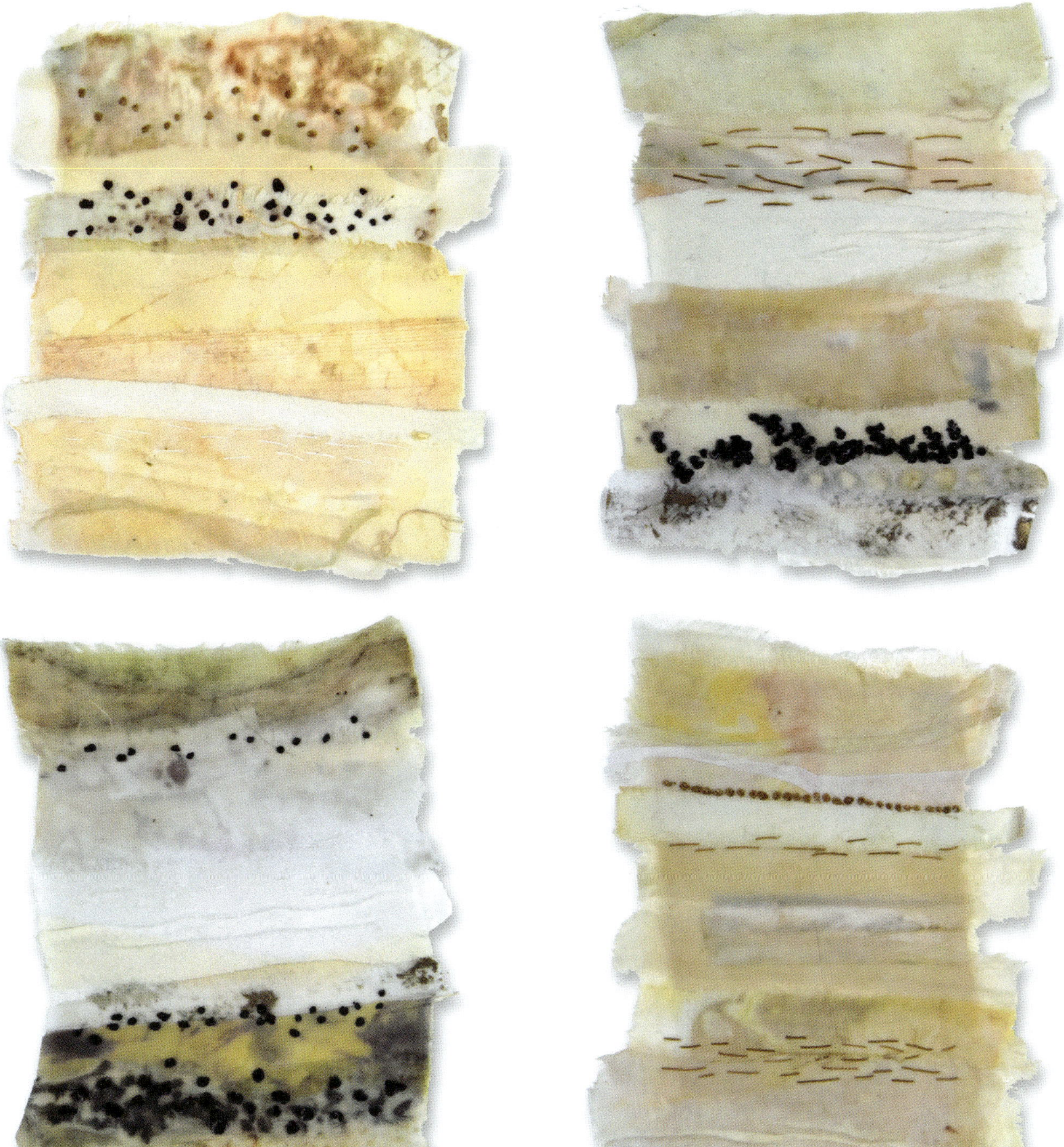

Botanically-dyed linen, cotton, and silk with stitch, 5" × 6" (13cm × 15cm)

FIELDS AGAIN

I've been obsessed with stitching field-like patterns again and decided to make a textile piece for each season.

WINTER

I started in winter and was thinking about all the layers below the fields and the generations who have worked the land. I started layering fabric and stitching with gold because of what is to come.

Twenty-five or thirty years ago, I was helping my dad plant his summer vegetable garden. I had just been to a psychology conference and was telling him about it. A topic at the conference was "transitions" and how it is best not to rush into something new but to be quiet for a while and slowly let the heart pull us in the new direction.

My wise and practical dad said, "Of course, it's just like in the garden. It needs a rest in winter."

We need winter to rest and to turn inward. All the hubbub of getting ready for Christmas is almost finished, and I am ready for the quiet of winter. The next few weeks will be filled with fires, good books, and gentle conversations. Slowly, new dreams for the coming year will emerge.

I was born in April, and I love the spring. But I will enjoy it more if I give myself some quiet time during the dormant winter months.

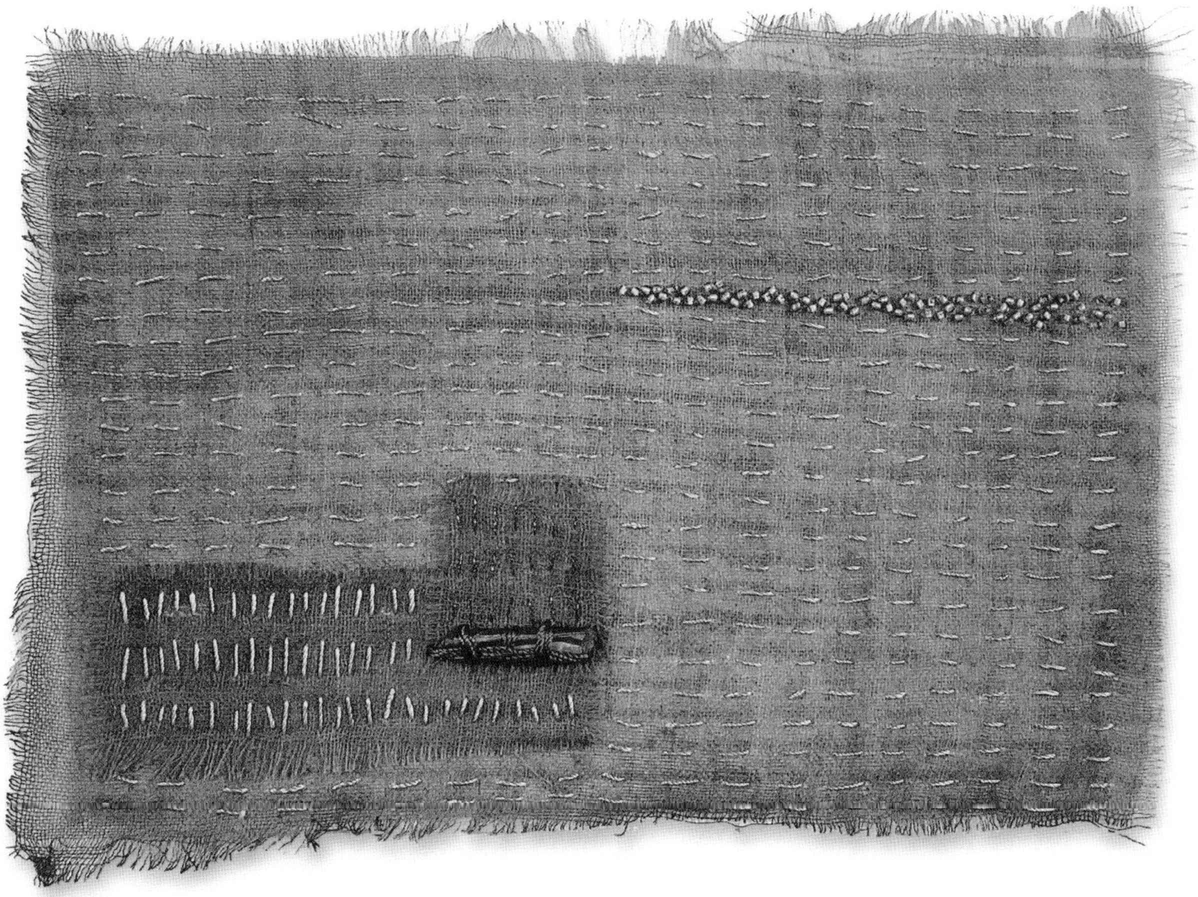

Winter
Hand-dyed wool, linen, canvas, silk and botanically-dyed paper; 9″ x 6″ (23cm ×15cm)

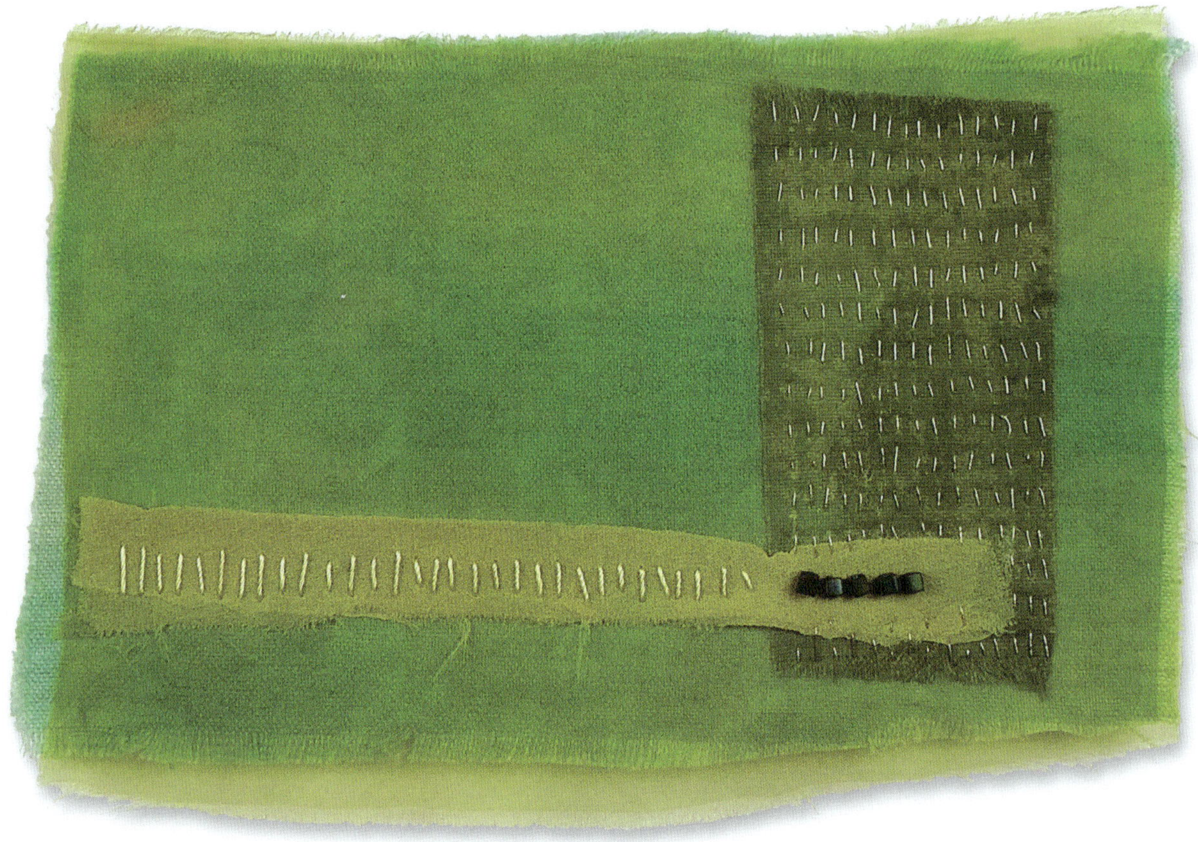

Spring
Hand-dyed wool, linen, canvas, silk and botanically-dyed paper; 9" x 6" (23cm ×15cm)

Spring

The fields are beginning to wake up; but spring isn't quite here yet. It's dark and rainy and way too cold after a much longer, colder, and wetter-than-normal winter. I feel that urge to begin awakening, but it isn't quite time. Impatience begins to bloom. Impatience, which has such a bad name, does have a purpose.

I imagine all those bulbs I planted the previous fall beginning to feel impatient as their urge to sprout grows. Likewise, the seemingly quiet fields have much happening underground that is as important as what is showing above the ground.

Finally, they unfurl. They push through the ground with force and begin to show their heads to the world.

Me, too. I am coming out of the cocoon of winter.

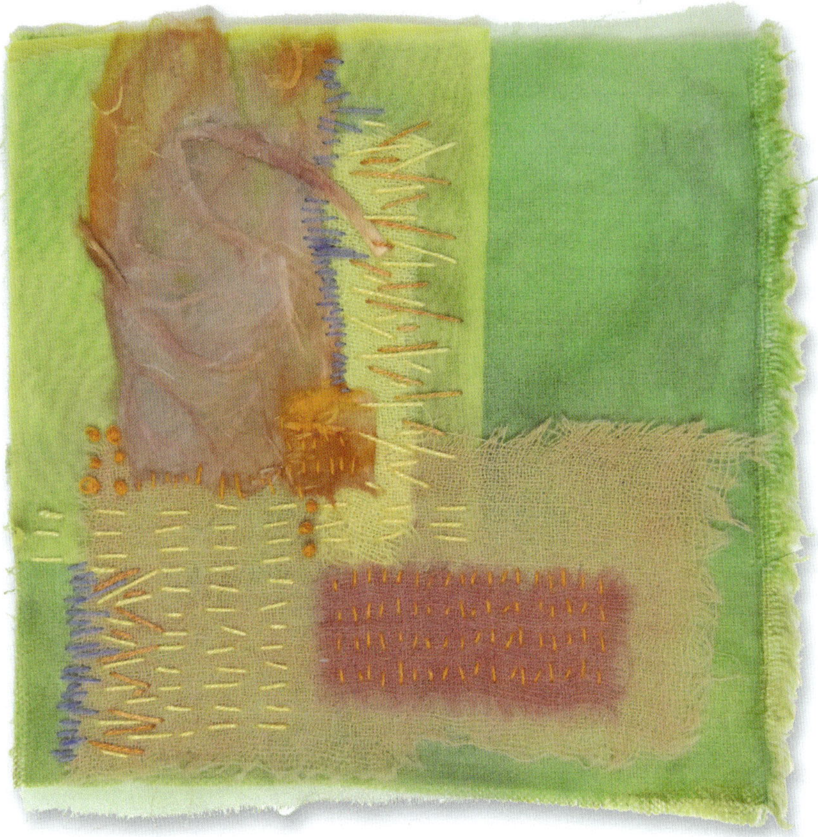

Summer
Hand-dyed wool, linen, canvas, silk and botanically-dyed paper; 9" x 6" (23cm ×15cm)

Summer

Summer is my least favorite season in the garden. My spring and fall gardens are the most beautiful and in summer they feel tired. Thank goodness, because it gives me time to ignore the garden and get out on the water in my kayak.

The first pieces I made for summer I didn't like. I think they knew I wasn't crazy about summer. Then I made this summer textile piece at the lake with my sister Kate and her husband, John, as slow time took over. It captures, for me, the bounty of summer, and maybe some of the laziness of a summer day. Nature is putting on a show, and we are only meant to sit back and enjoy it.

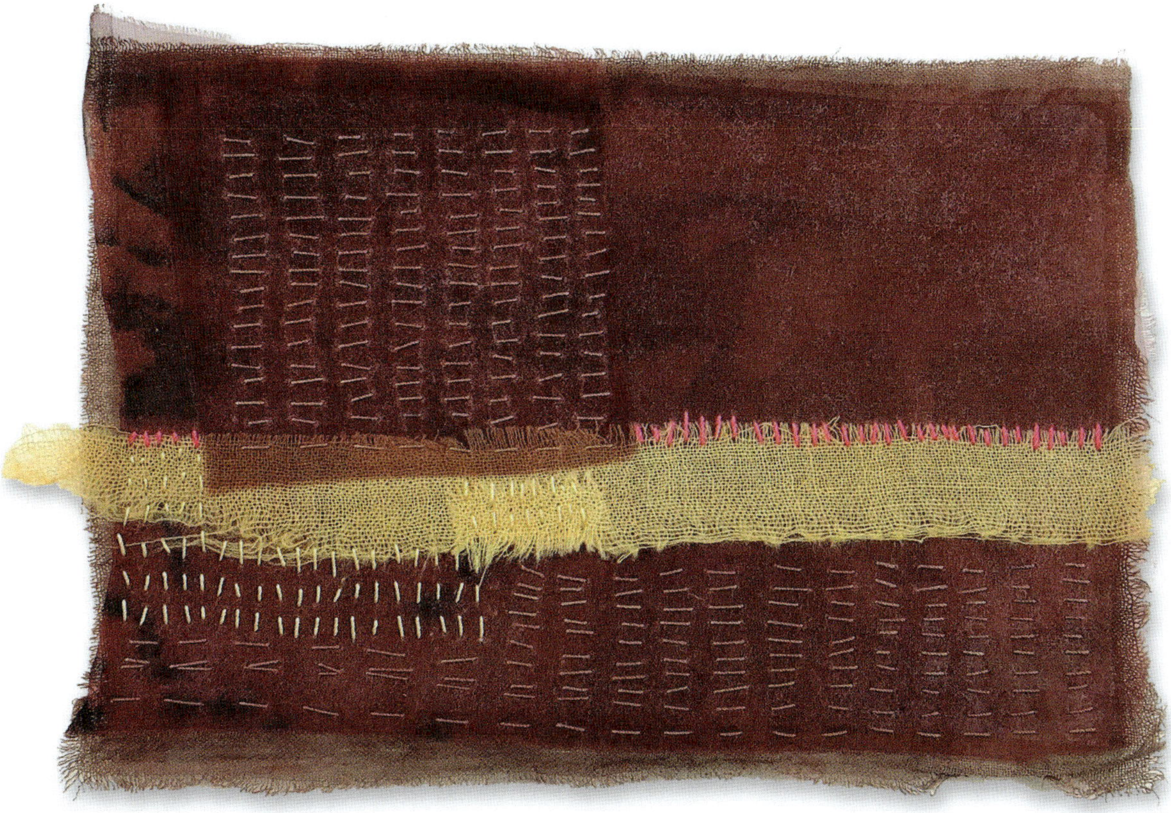

Autumn
Hand-dyed wool, linen, canvas, silk and botanically-dyed paper; 9″ x 6″ (23cm ×15cm)

Autumn

In fall, it's the riotous colors that thrill me. My Japanese maples display the most gorgeous colors. I begin to think about the approaching winter and the time for renewal. I try to get the last things done that I wanted to do this year and then watch as the year fades away in a last blast of glory.

LOVE

I recently finished a piece that I love. It is so gentle; I can almost see the soft snowbanks covering a North Dakota field.

Some pieces I am so tired of by the time I finish them that I don't love them anymore. Sometimes, it is only years later that I look at them again and love them anew.

But not this piece. I am in love with it now. I want to give it all the time it needs so that it can be the most beautiful piece it can be. I stitch a tiny filament thread into the field stamp that most people will never see; but I will. It shimmers . . . like a glittering snow-covered field.

It's days like this, love like this, that keep me working away in the studio.

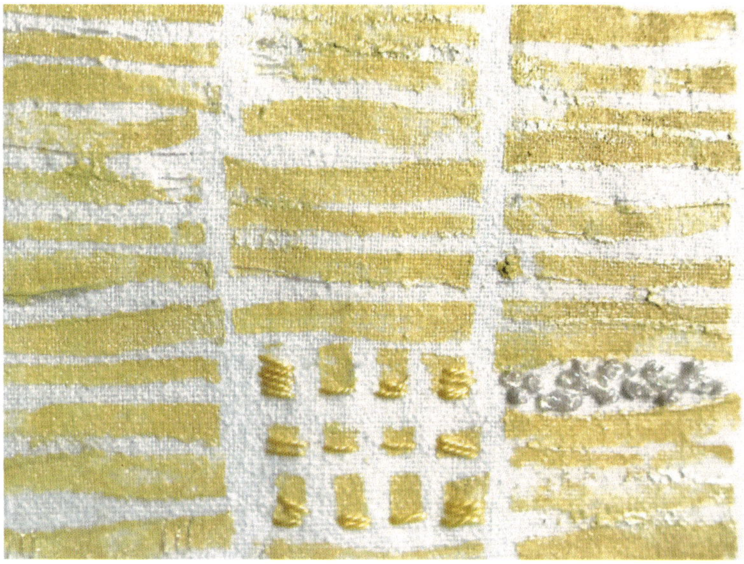

Here's a close-up so you can see it, too.

I should not be calling this piece "it" anymore but "her." She has her own being now, separate from me. As Vally used to say, "Once a piece is born, you don't have the right to be careless with it. It has its own life."

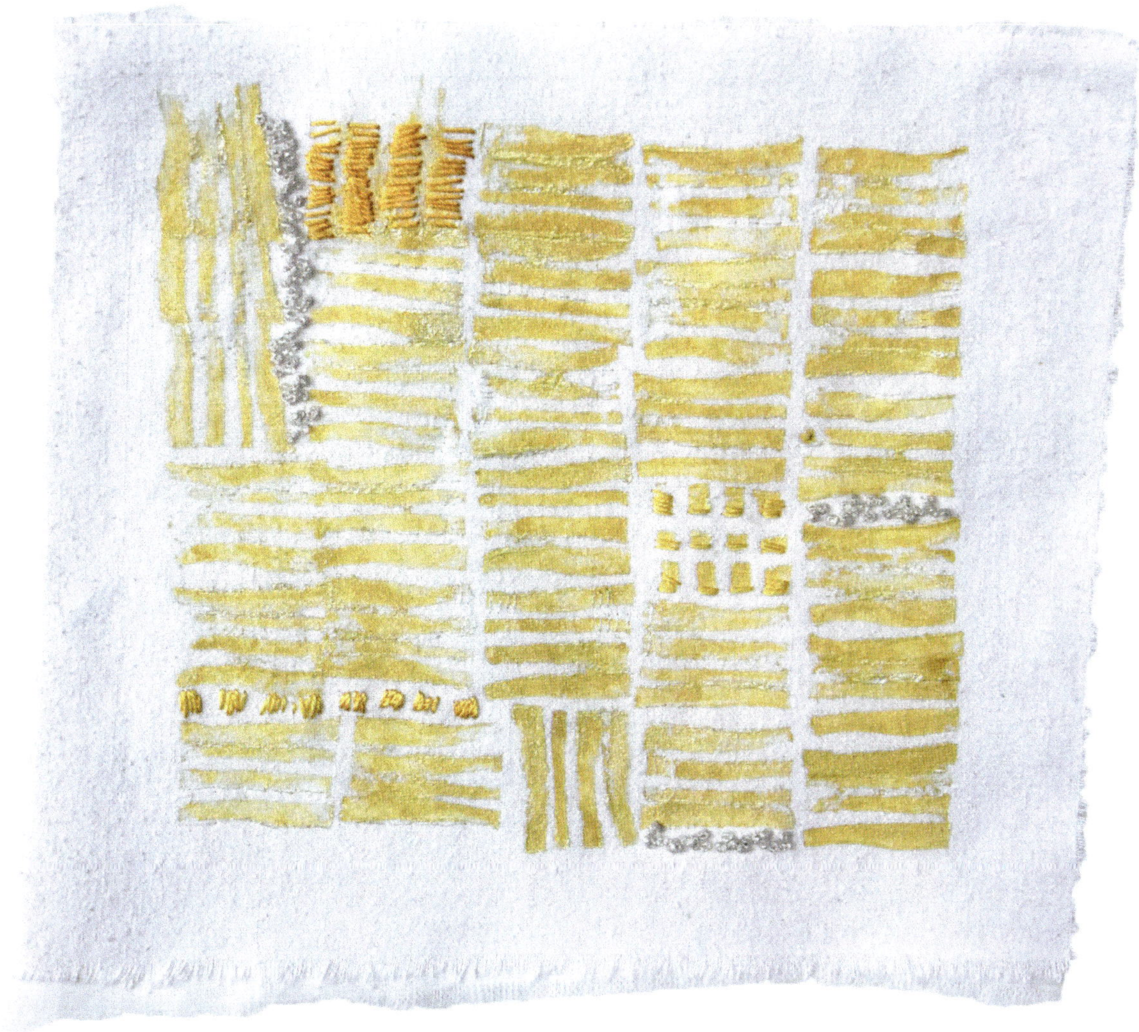

Love
Layers of silk and linen, paint, stitch, and beads. 8" × 8" (20cm ×20cm)

GRANPI'S GARDEN

As I slowly put together a new field piece, I remember the first field that I loved. My Granpi Silvis's vegetable garden covered about an acre on his land that fronted Sugar Lake in Minnesota. That land, the vegetable garden, and the times spent at "the lake" are my best memories of growing up. We lived about an hour from the lake and would spend countless weekends there with my cousins, aunts, and uncles. With six aunts, five uncles, and twenty-three cousins, that was often a crowd.

The best times for me were waking up early with Granpi before anyone else was up. We'd walk down to the lake to go fishing as the sun rose. We'd often catch enough sunnies to feed everyone at lunch. If we caught catfish, he said they made the best garden fertilizer, and we'd save a few for that. After cleaning the sunnies, we'd bury the remains and the catfish "where the garden needed a little help." Then, we'd walk around the whole garden pulling a few weeds here and there as we went. He used to say, "Gardens don't take a lot of work, but they take a lot of looking."

By then we were hot, and we'd race to the lake for a cool dip. All this happened before most of the household even stirred. It's probably why I love early mornings so much.

Those days have left me with a sense of wonder about what is buried beneath the earth. I wonder what is growing in his old garden now and if the remnants of his old rows still show through on the contour of the land. And what about the decades and centuries before he farmed that land?

I want to honor those prior happenings on the land, so I layer fabrics and then layer some more to create that sense of history.

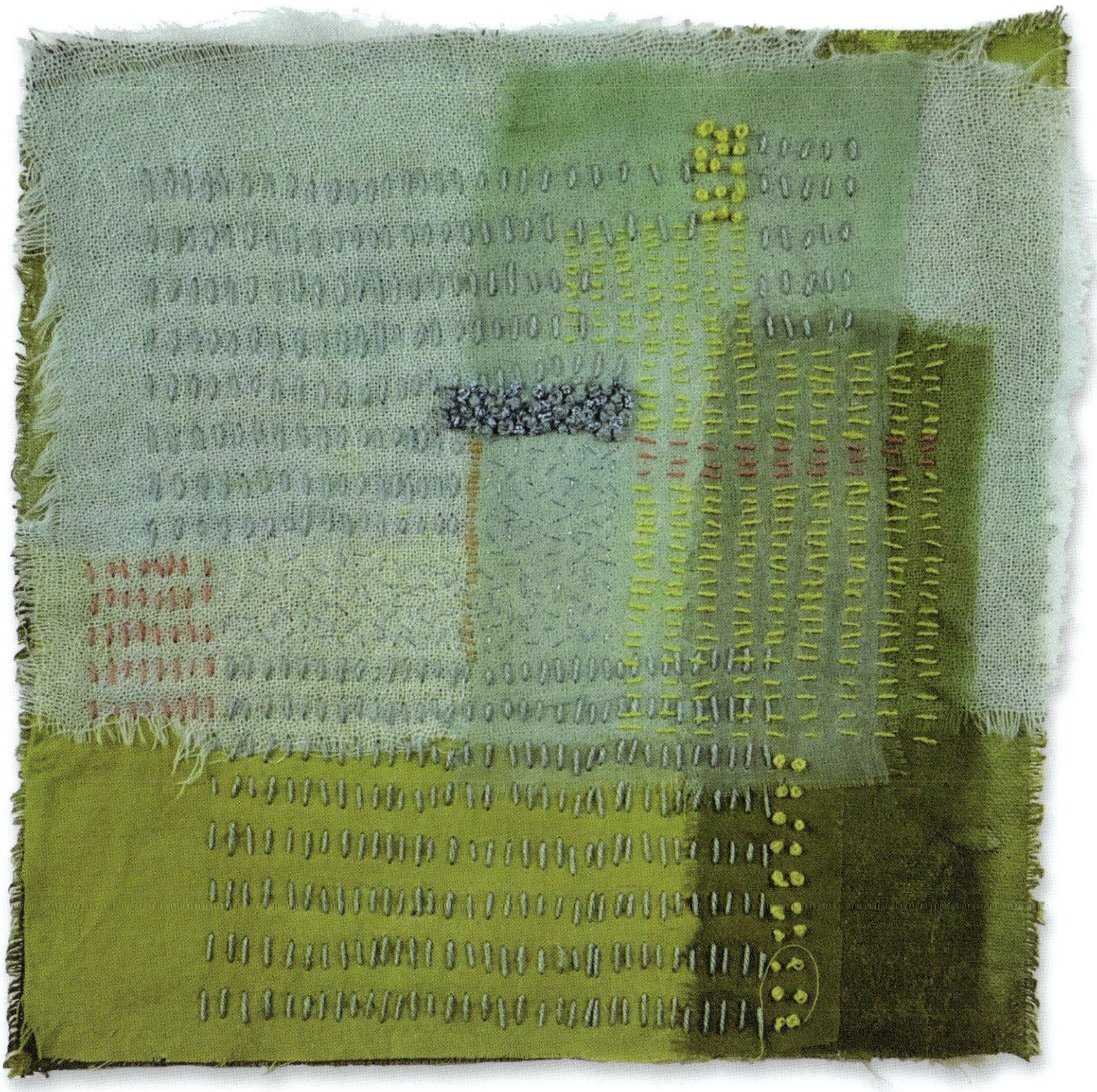

Granpi's Garden
Wool, cotton, silk, and stitch, 8" × 8" (20cm ×20cm)

PAST WORK

Sometimes, looking back on my life, I gloss over transgressions and embarrassments. Even with photos and keepsakes, it's hard to accurately remember the emotions and tenor of the moment.

Not so with old art journals.

One day, as I was "wandering" through my old art journals, I came upon one from thirty years earlier that I hadn't looked at in years. I was so embarrassed. The pieces in it were sticky sweet and the color palate too soft and gentle. Was I ever that naive? Clearly so. Ugh.

I decided to throw it away lest anyone see those early, unsophisticated attempts at expression.

Those clumsy attempts at art reminded me of embarrassing moments in my life when my response was inappropriate or lacking in emotional depth and empathy—like not responding with generosity when a beloved sister asked for help years ago.
I understand now how hard it is to have to ask for help; I wish I had known that then.

I wonder what I am making in my studio now that will seem trite and ill-conceived in thirty years. I wonder what actions I am taking now that will seem immature and lacking in grace and wisdom later.

This is what I know, though: it took vulnerability and courage to start making art. It took vulnerability and courage to try to make a life that fits me—the me who loves variety and freedom.

So, I say to the young woman who started an art journal, "Good job. You'll get better." And I say to the younger me who was foolish or unkind, "You're getting better. You're learning."

Maybe I should keep that old art journal after all. Nah, it's going out. I've moved on.

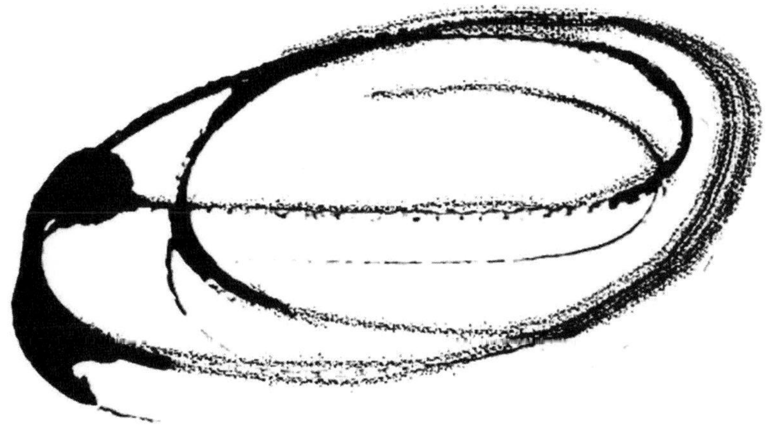

ETHEREAL

I love it when a piece I am making has an ethereal quality, because I like to think about art as a way to bring the divine to Earth. One time I set out to create a series of pieces with that idea as the inspiration behind them.

However, the more I tried to create that feeling, the more it disappeared. Like a wisp of smoke, the feeling faded into the atmosphere and the piece lacked substance and felt trite.

Then, on another of my daily walks, I saw the sun backlighting a plum tree so that its purplish leaves became luminescent. A neighbor's puppy, with its playful exuberance, made me laugh. The sun hit the water and sparkled. I thought, "The divine is all around us, in the substance of the things we love." If I try too hard to make a piece ethereal, it loses that substance. It is the marriage of the divine and Earth that makes my heart, and my art, sing.

Sometimes an idea grabs hold of spontaneity and playfulness in its determination. Playfulness and intuition are the better course for me. Sing a little, dance a little, and something better might come along. A piece just falls together that has the qualities I love.

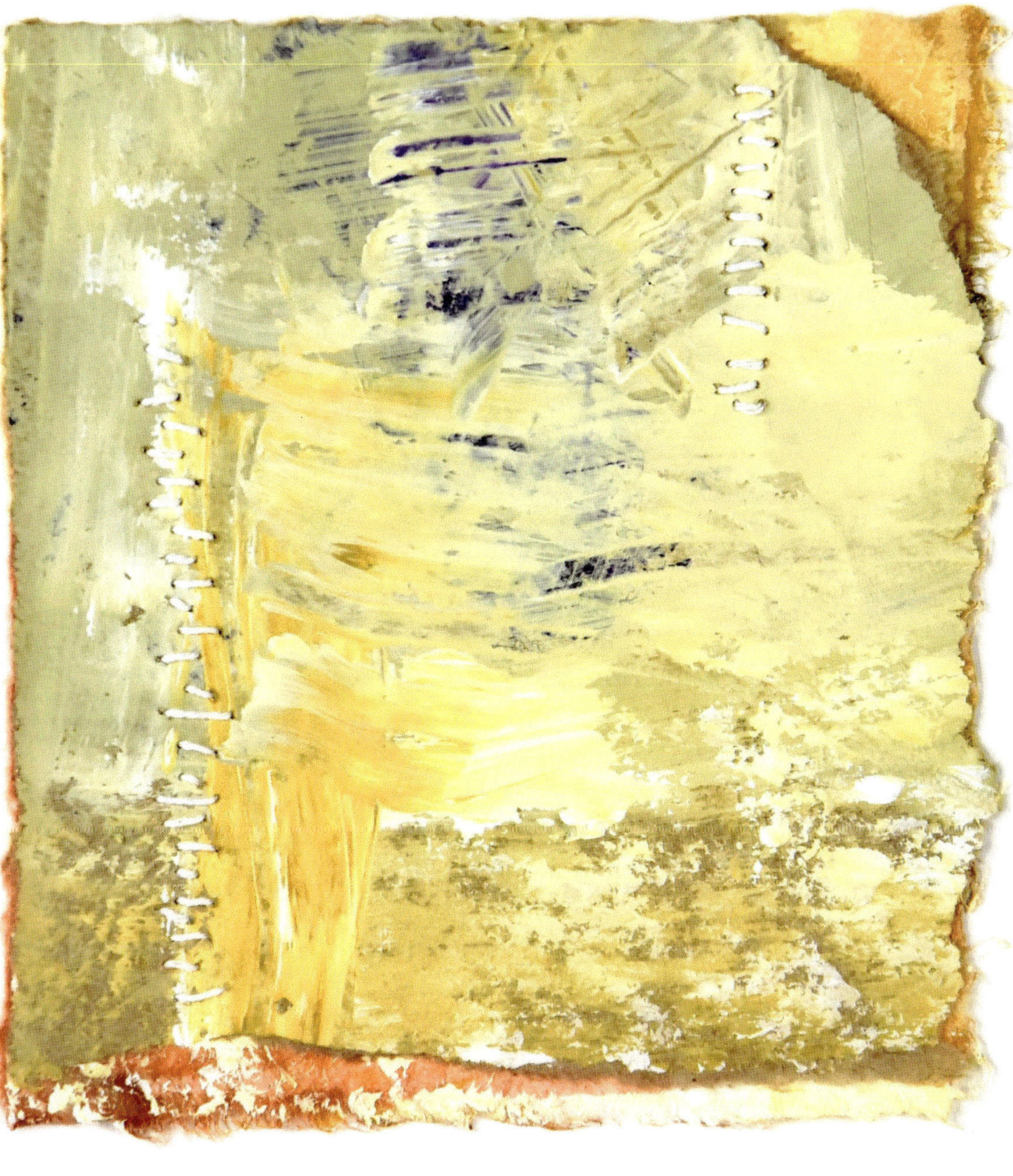

Morning Haze
Washi paper collage with stitch, 7″ x 8″ (18cm x 20cm)

FRAGMENTS

I was working on a larger textile piece and one segment was just wrong. I had already done a lot of stitching on it, and I kept trying to think of how to incorporate it in the rest of the piece. I have learned from experience that sometimes when you figure out how to incorporate a mistake into a piece, it becomes the strongest part of the piece. By having to solve the challenge, something new and even better can emerge.

Well, that was not happening with this piece. Nothing seemed to make it work.

I am used to cutting up paper to make smaller pieces, but I had never cut up stitched pieces and pieced them back together in a new way. I bravely cut through the fabric and the stitch and made a new piece.

Huh . . . kind of fun. I liked it again. Once more, courage and trust can show me the way.

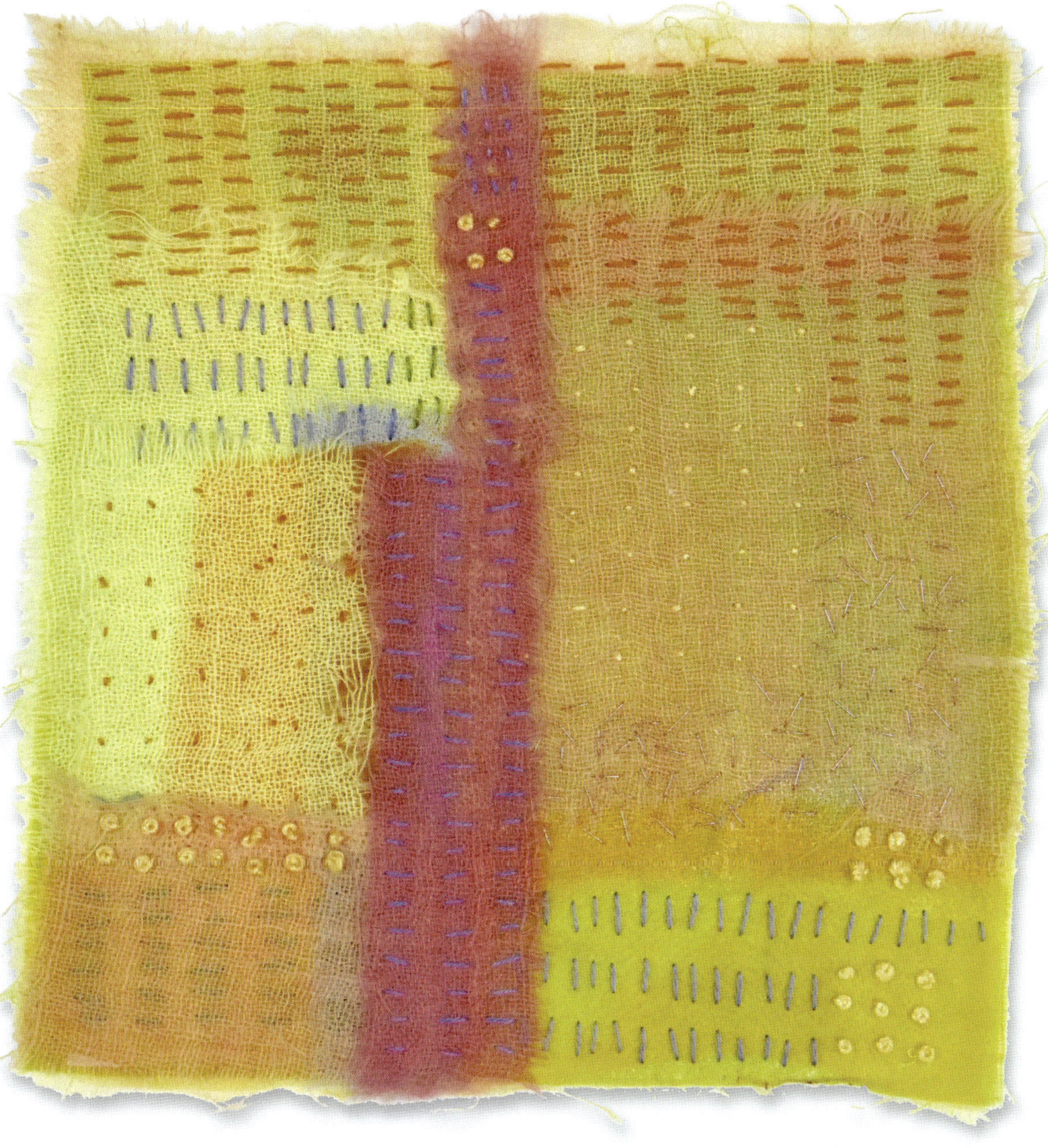

Pastel Fields
Hand-dyed linens, silk and wool with stitch; 6" × 6" (15cm × 15cm);
Can you see where I have stitched over prior stitches?

PARALLEL

Bruce took a couple of terrible falls several years ago and was confined to a wheelchair for three months. He needed me. As I took over a caregiver role, my days became more structured in order to fit everything in.

The squares of the field pieces accommodated that need for more structure. I liked the rows and the squarish blocks. They seemed to anchor me. I still love the field pieces, but when Bruce recovered, I found myself wanting less control again, more serendipity.

My artwork so often parallels what is happening in my life. When I'm relaxed and carefree, my artwork has that feel. When I am disciplined and controlled, my artwork looks disciplined and controlled. Sometimes, the artwork is a harbinger of times ahead.

As I look at this piece, I think things are about to change. It's looser.

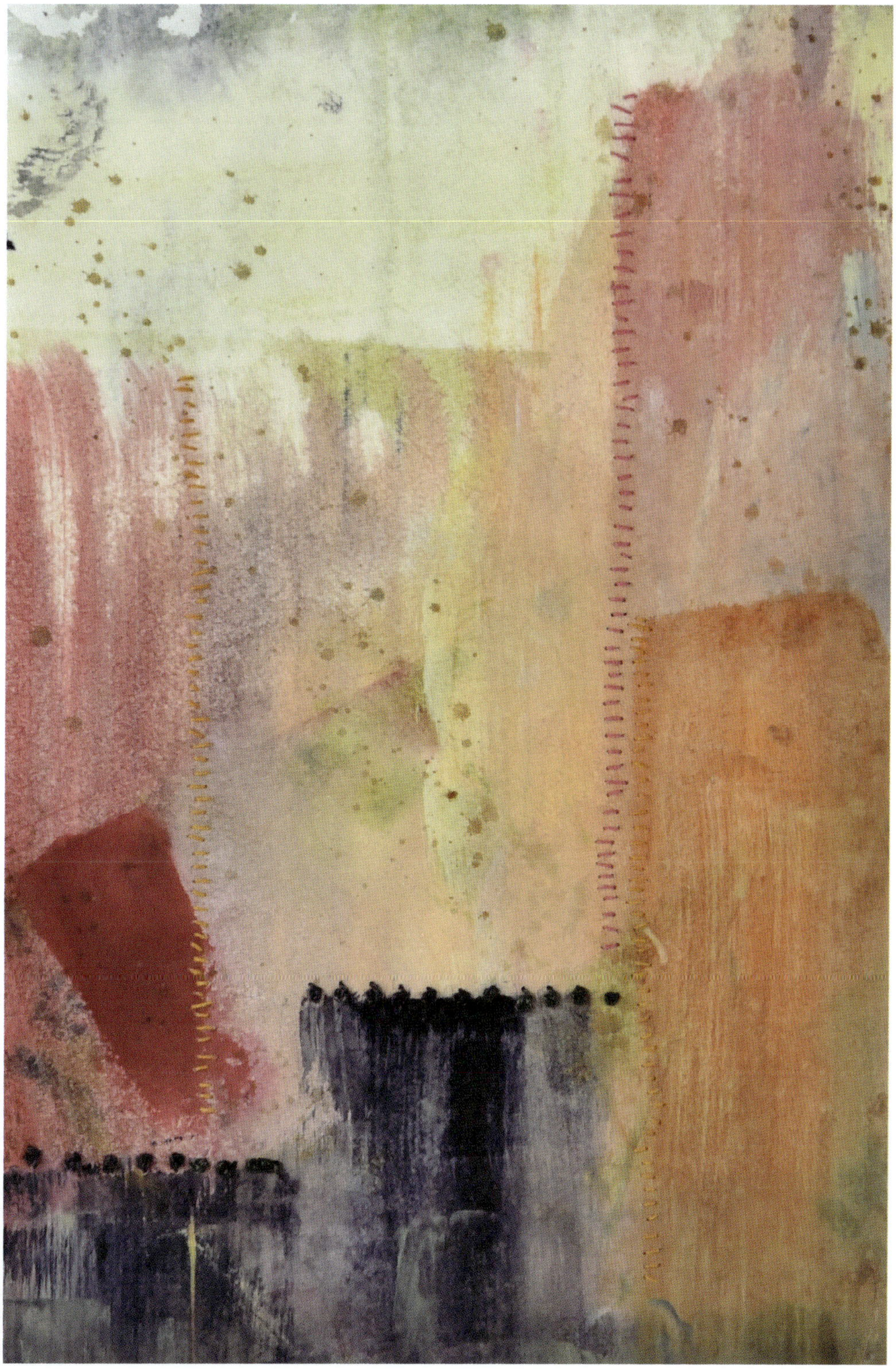

Parallels
Washi paper with acrylic, inks, and stitch, 6" x 9" (15cm x 23cm)

A LONG LIFE

On New Year's Eve I usually take time to intuit about the year ahead. What might it hold for me? What are my responsibilities? Each year seems to have its own color, its own temperament. Sometimes I feel it is a year to explore or to widen horizons or to find the spotlight.

I think about the characteristics of different years and times in my life and the life of others as I work on a new piece called "A Long Life." I am piecing together field-like segments that are reminiscent of the segments in our lives.

In some segments I was blissfully free, like when I lived in Topanga, California. In others, I was consumed with work, kept my head down and did the work. In others, like when I studied with Jean Houston, I was expanding horizons. As I work on this long-life piece, I think about all those segments that are buried in me, still part of me but not always visible to others.

We are all more than what we see on the surface.

Just like the land. When Bruce and I lived in Virginia, we lived on ground that witnessed Civil War battles. Surely, those land memories must have emanated from the soil.

Layers and layers—in everything.

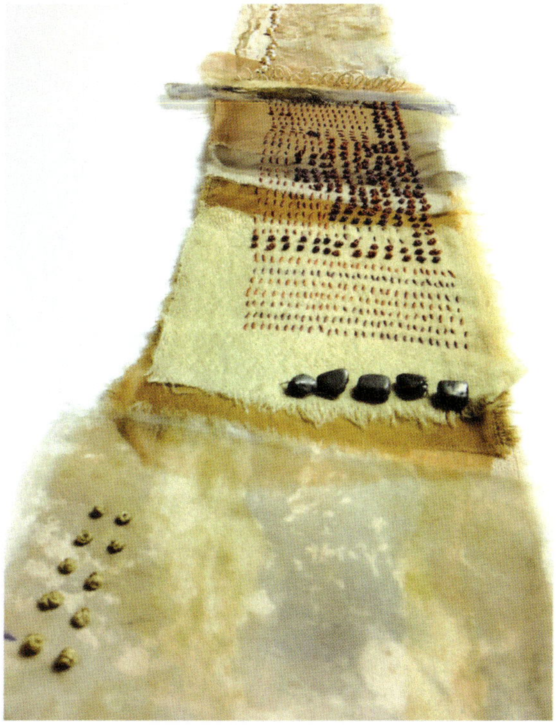

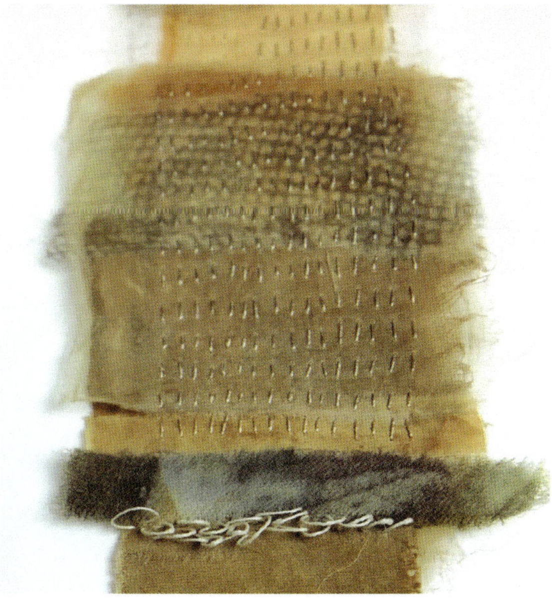

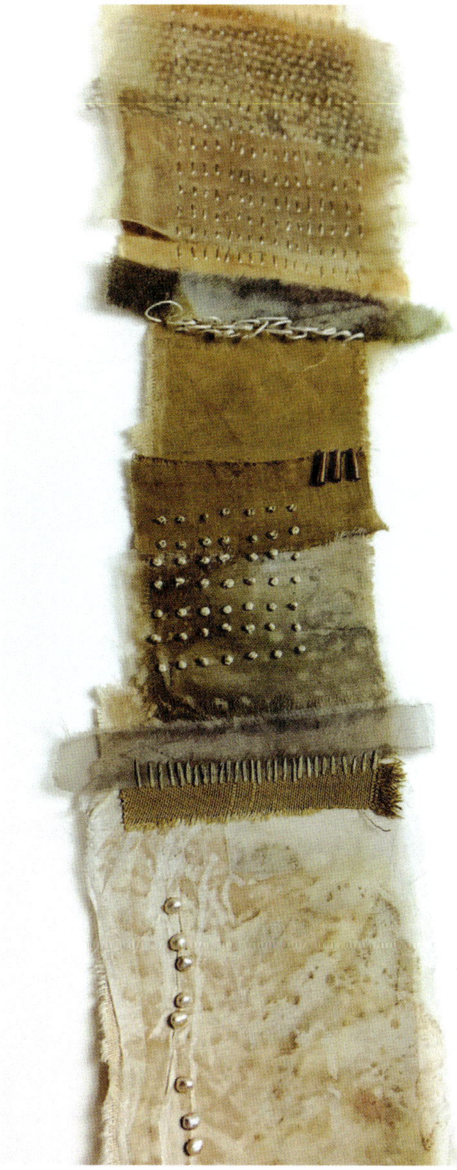

A Long Life
Botanically-dyed wool, canvas, silk and linen with stitch; 3.5" × 42" (9cm × 107cm)

LETTING GO

I love to finish things. It feels so good to finish a piece of art; clear some physical, emotional, and mental space; and have the freedom that comes between projects. That could be partly why I like making small pieces so much. Large pieces with a lot of "slow stitch" take forever to finish.

Sometimes a bigger project will hold my interest for months at a time; sometimes I have to recognize that it no longer has my heart and give up on it. My heart has to be in it, or it loses that spark, that sense of wonder that I think moves into and touches the work.

I had to abandon a big project recently. I realized that I was grinding through the motions using determination instead of passion to propel me forward. And, my studio had become a mess as I worked on this piece.

So, I put the project away, and the entire space felt light again and ready for play.

The experience reminded me that there are times in life, too, when we have to shift directions. Seventeen years ago, Bruce and I bought our first home in Gig Harbor, Washington. I loved that house, and its gardens, worked tirelessly on both, and loved them as a result. But there were a lot of stairs at that house, and, while Bruce could handle the stairs when we bought the house, we quickly discovered that Parkinson's disease and stairs don't go together. One day when I was out in the garden, a strong intuition came to me that it was time to let go. We listed the house within a week. It was scary, but I continued to feel it was the right thing to do.

But we found a home that I loved even more. More importantly, there are no stairs into the house, and the master bedroom is on the main floor. As Bruce's Parkinson's progressed, having no stairs was critical and meant that we could easily get in and out of the house. I was glad we took that leap; I still am.

I remember that today as I clean up my studio and put the big project away.

RETROSPECTIVES

Change keeps us from getting stuck and becoming rigid. It's exciting, annoying, and part of life.

Not long ago, I was loving the pieces I made. And then, all of a sudden, I got bored and wanted to try new things. What a bother that can be! I'd like to go back to my fields, but I feel called to try something different for a while. And so, it begins again.

I've come to think that certain of my art pieces or styles have their time, and when that time is over, I can't go back. I sometimes wish I could make pieces in an earlier style, but they become formulas and feel tight and boring. It's like my hands and heart have changed and the DNA is no longer there for that kind of work.

I know this happens to others, too. I sometimes wish other artists would make hundreds of pieces in a style that I love, but they inevitably move on to something new. We can only cherish the few that they made when their DNA was in place for that.

This process of continually stepping into the unknown, trusting that a new path will emerge is essential for growth and art.

This is at least partially why I like to see retrospectives of other artists' work; I like to see the path they traveled in their artistic evolution. With many artists, you can see their original imprint even when they change mediums and styles.

Our core is still there, but the expression has shifted.

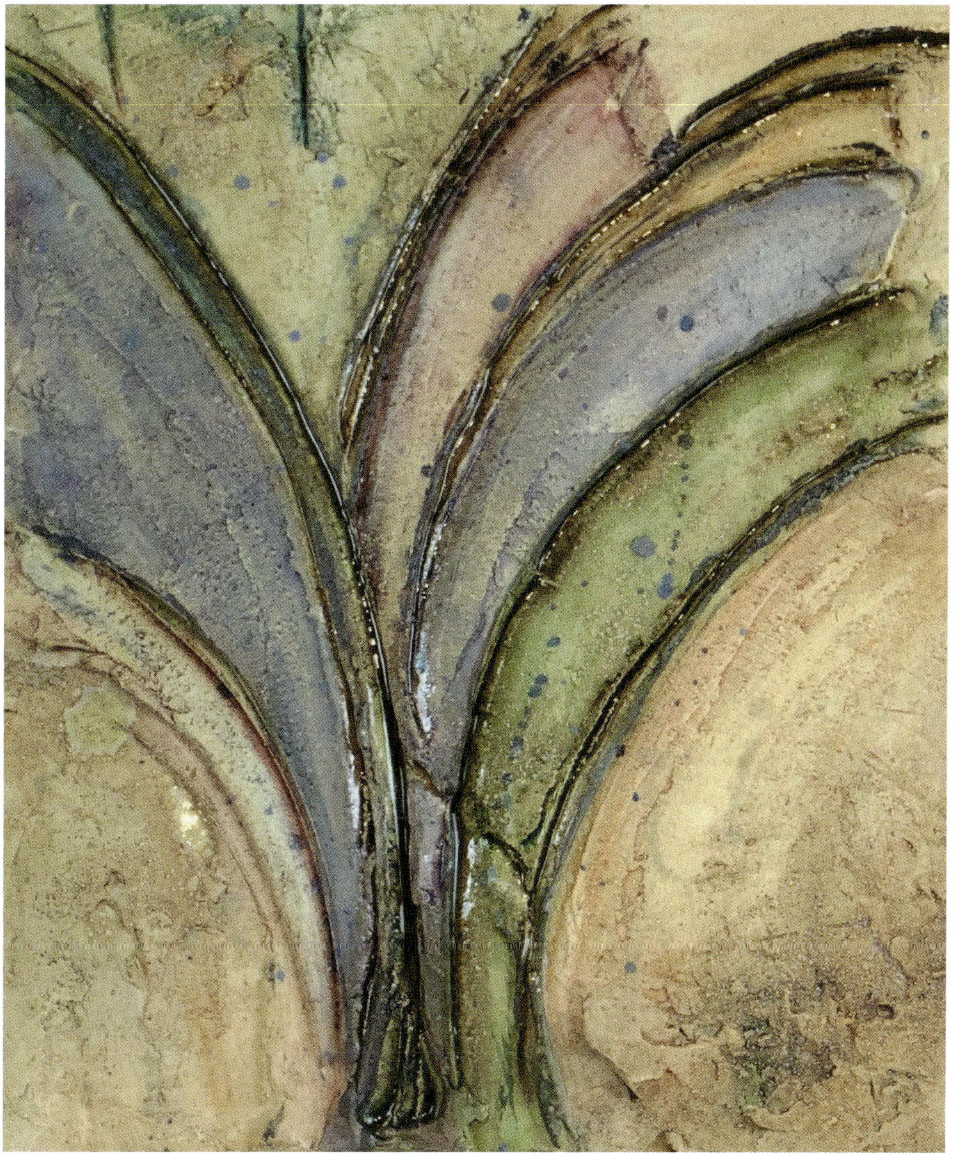

Growth
This gesture shows up in my artwork again and again. Remember one of those first paintings I showed Vally on page 41? I made this stoneware tile piece decades later. 12.5" × 15" (32cm × 38cm)

THE IN-BETWEEN

As the process of change begins, there is usually a period where nothing feels right and, like the fields I love, I need to lie fallow for a time to see what will emerge. I call them my in-between times. Still, it's good to have something creative to do when I am in one of those times. For me, at least this time, it is canning—chutneys, jams, jellies, vinegars, and vegetables.

I started canning because I loved the look of a canning cupboard. I know that is a crazy reason to do canning, but I am so visual and seeing jars lined up, full of jewel tones, excites me.

It's the middle of winter and that's not the best time to can, but it isn't slowing me down. I love making chutneys. I've made a cranberry, carrot, and apricot chutney. I've made an orange and lemon marmalade and a sweet red pepper jelly. I wonder how many more I will make before I can go back to art.

The canning cupboard now looks beautiful.

I would think it was crazier except that Vally once said to me to make sure that my containers in the refrigerator looked appealing and beautiful. She always used her wonderful pottery for leftovers.

If you are rolling your eyes, don't worry, I am, too.

Artists are a strange breed. Sometimes we are just meant to do the impractical so that our souls sing again. And the perfect time for that is the in-between.

I should say, though, that canning is not impractical. I now have easy ways to make everyday meals that satisfy. A small jar of apricot chutney spread over chicken breasts bakes in twenty minutes. With rice cooking and broccoli steaming, I quickly have a nutritious and interesting meal to put on the table.

Sweet red pepper jelly on top of cream cheese, and I have a good appetizer for surprise guests.

Pear compote over vanilla ice cream, and an easy dessert comes together.

But . . . it's not why I started canning.

More of the In-Between

Another in-between activity for me is gardening. Just as winter is not the best time for canning, it's also not the best time to garden. But winter is a great time to plan gardens, and I like that. I am consumed with how to make a garden at my new home. I am slowly beginning to build the kind of garden I love.

I always want paths in my garden so that I can move through it each day. It's a little harder here because the lot is very narrow. It is also on a steep bank that goes down to the water; however, I've been able to make a loop with the path to the water as part of the journey. I'm finding my way.

The poor land here, though. In the past, trees have been sawed off at six feet to keep the view. Blackberries and English ivy would like to cover everything.

I am reading and thinking about how to heal the land. I'm researching which plants I can sneak into this steep bank that will help hold the soil and create a tapestry of color. It's engrossing and allows me to leave the studio alone until I know what to do next.

And More of the In-Between

At the library one day, while thinking about gardens, I spotted a copy of *Gardens of the High Line* by Piet Oudolf and Rick Darke. The High Line is a New York City garden built along old railroad tracks. It's a walking garden with an emphasis on sustainability and ecology. I've known about this garden for a while, but this book brought it all home. It calls to me, and I am dying to see it.

But I had so many responsibilities. Bruce needed help again; the house, the garden, and clients all needed me. But I got to thinking about how I could pull off a trip. To be in New York City again would be a bit of heaven for me: to feel the energy of the streets, to see an Alvin Ailey performance, to walk the High Line, to go to museums and galleries.

I begin dancing again, too. I feel the bigger world again.

As I thought about going to New York, though, I remembered all the good times Bruce and I have had in New York. I don't want to go without him.

Still, from our couch, I can feel that larger world again and it has left me dancing.

MOVING ON

Finally, it has happened. It started because I thought I would go ahead and dye some fabric scraps that had been soaking in soda ash for months just so that I could clean up my studio space.

Oh, the colors that came out of the dye pot, pale lime and turquoise, light grays and lilacs, a few gorgeous soft greens. I swooned. The colors reminded me of a time almost thirty years ago when Bruce and I drove up to the mountains from Salt Lake City and stopped at a clearing. The short grasses of the meadow in the winter light became the most beautiful shades of lime and ice blue. I thought at the time that to be able to capture those colors someday would be pure joy.

The newly dyed fabric was lying on my worktable all in a jumble. The pieces seemed to fly together into a series of about fifteen 5" × 7" (13cm × 18cm) pieces that I call "Quiet Morning." I finished the first one in a few hours with a simple "stitch in the field pattern." They were quieter, softer, more meditative.

I loved them.

It's not what my mind wanted to do next. My mind was thinking about circles and curvy lines and more grays and blacks.

It reminded me of a time I went to hear a potter speak about her work. I wish so much I could remember her name but, sadly, I don't. She made these delightful little majolica cups, saucers, and plates that had a wild, wonderful, and fun mixture of color and pattern. They reminded me of the Matisse cutouts. She started her slideshow with photos of the artists I love: Rothko, Motherwell, and other minimalists. She said, "I love this work. I wish I could make it. But I grew up around Victorian houses." And she showed slides of colorful, patterned detail that you see on Victorian homes. She went on to say that she tries to do that minimalist, powerfully quiet work but her hand always creates the detailed, playful patterns.

And so it is with me. At least for now, fields are what my hands want to make. Those curvy blacks and greys may come alive at some point. But I've learned it often takes a period of gestation before that new form will emerge.

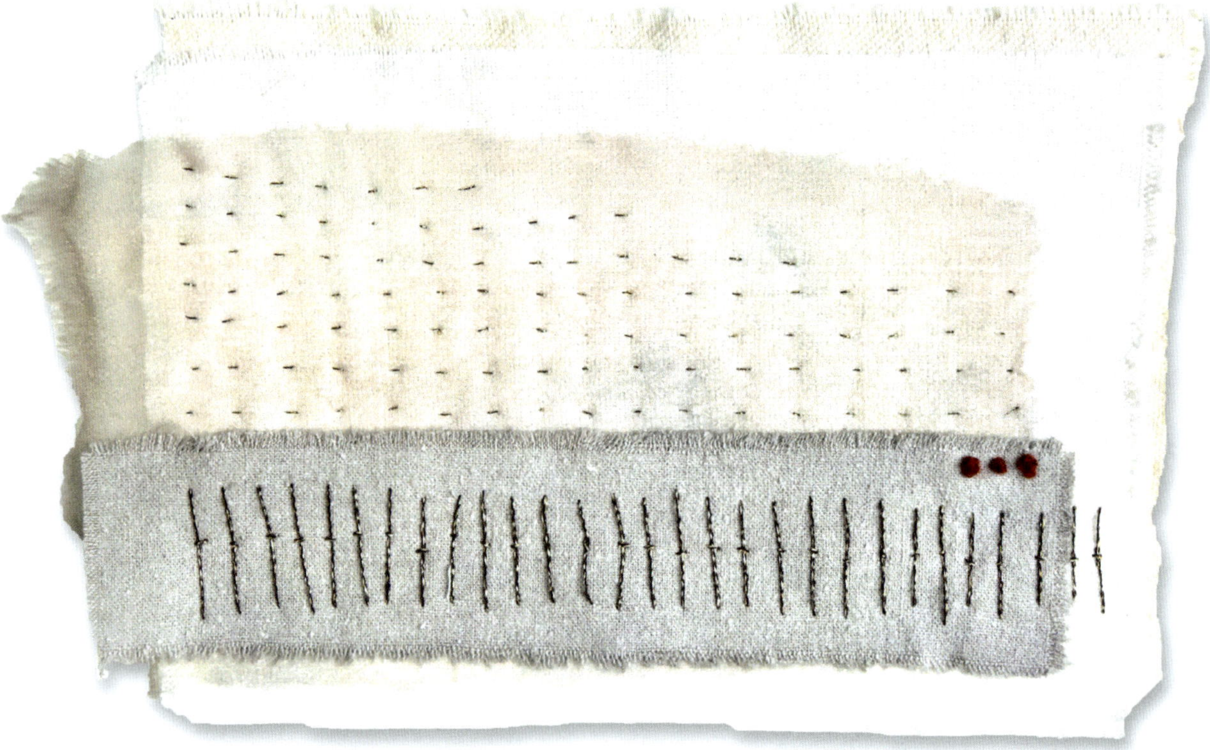

Quiet Morning series
Collage of hand-dyed fabrics and stitch, 8" × 5" (20cm ×13cm)

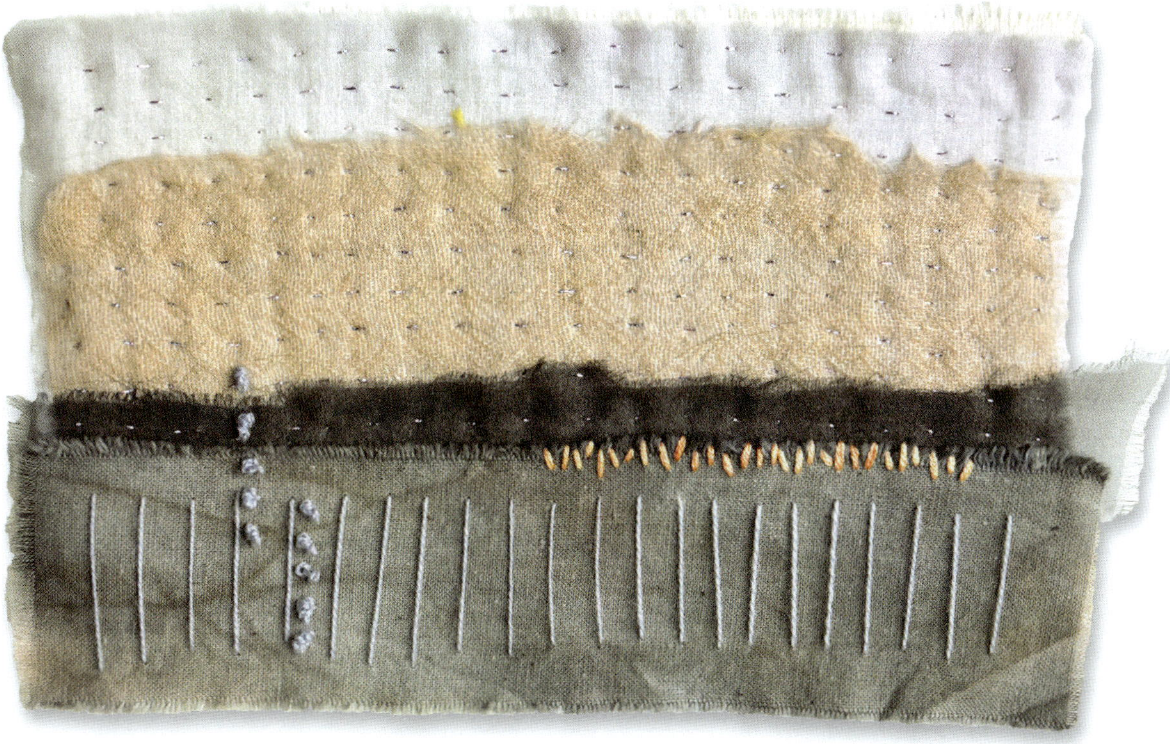

FRUSTRATION

I finished the "Quiet Morning" series. I loved making it. But then what? Nothing I tried seemed to capture my heart. I was so frustrated that I was ready to give up on art all together. I kept trying to paint on canvas the way I paint on paper and would make a terrible mess. I looked around knowing that I still had to clean up the whole mess.

For a few short days, I felt the freedom that I would have if I wasn't always trying to make art. I thought of all the things that I would then have time for: more people, more garden walks, more reading, a dog, and relaxing.

I sighed with relief. I could let it go and just do other things with the rest of my life. That was a new feeling for me, because I have never really thought of giving up on art.

And then, for the first time in months, I had an intuitive flash of how to work with fabric in a way that would capture my vision. I started using a combination of acrylic paint and dye on canvas and it worked. I was in love again.

Someone—I wish I could remember who—said that we should see more of the work of renowned artists that isn't so good. They all have pieces like that. Even Renoir had a period that was lackluster. Dr. Barnes didn't buy any of those paintings.

It might give all of us a bit more confidence and persistence to know that frustration is a necessary part of the process.

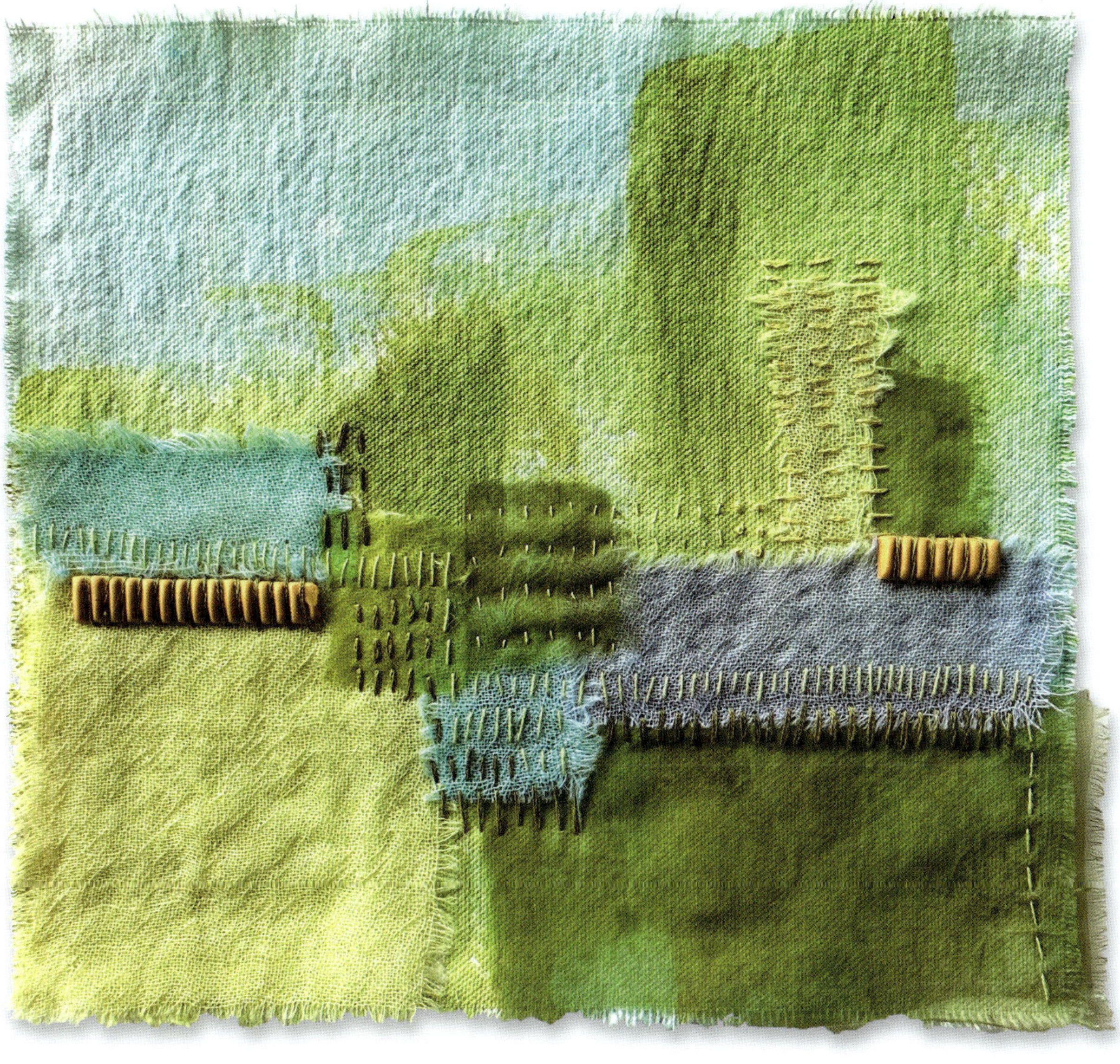

Fields Again
Collage of acrylic on canvas, hand-dyed cotton, wool, and silk with handmade polymer beads, 8″ × 8″ (20cm × 20cm)

EVOLUTION

It's been five years since I switched to textiles and mixed media from clay. My practice is deepening. When I first switched, it was a new love—exciting and exuberant. Now the love is quieter, steadier, deeper.

I've been learning to dye with plants. It feels so close to the earth. The colors are softer and remind me of the garden. It's fun doing the tests; it reminds me of the years I spent doing glaze tests.

As I stitch, I am listening to *The Hidden Life of Trees: What They Feel, How They Communicate—Discoveries from a Secret World* by Peter Wohlleben. I notice plants more now and wonder how they contribute to the ecosystem. Textiles are leading me back to the garden.

I want to paint with botanical dyes someday. And then stitch with botanically-dyed threads. I would love to grow the plants that I use for dyes.

I find being out-of-doors more important, especially in wild places with long vistas. I am more likely to just sit in such places and let the wisdom of the Earth, the plants, the critters, and the birds calm me.

Bringing little bits of that to my art feels like my home; it feels like Vally.

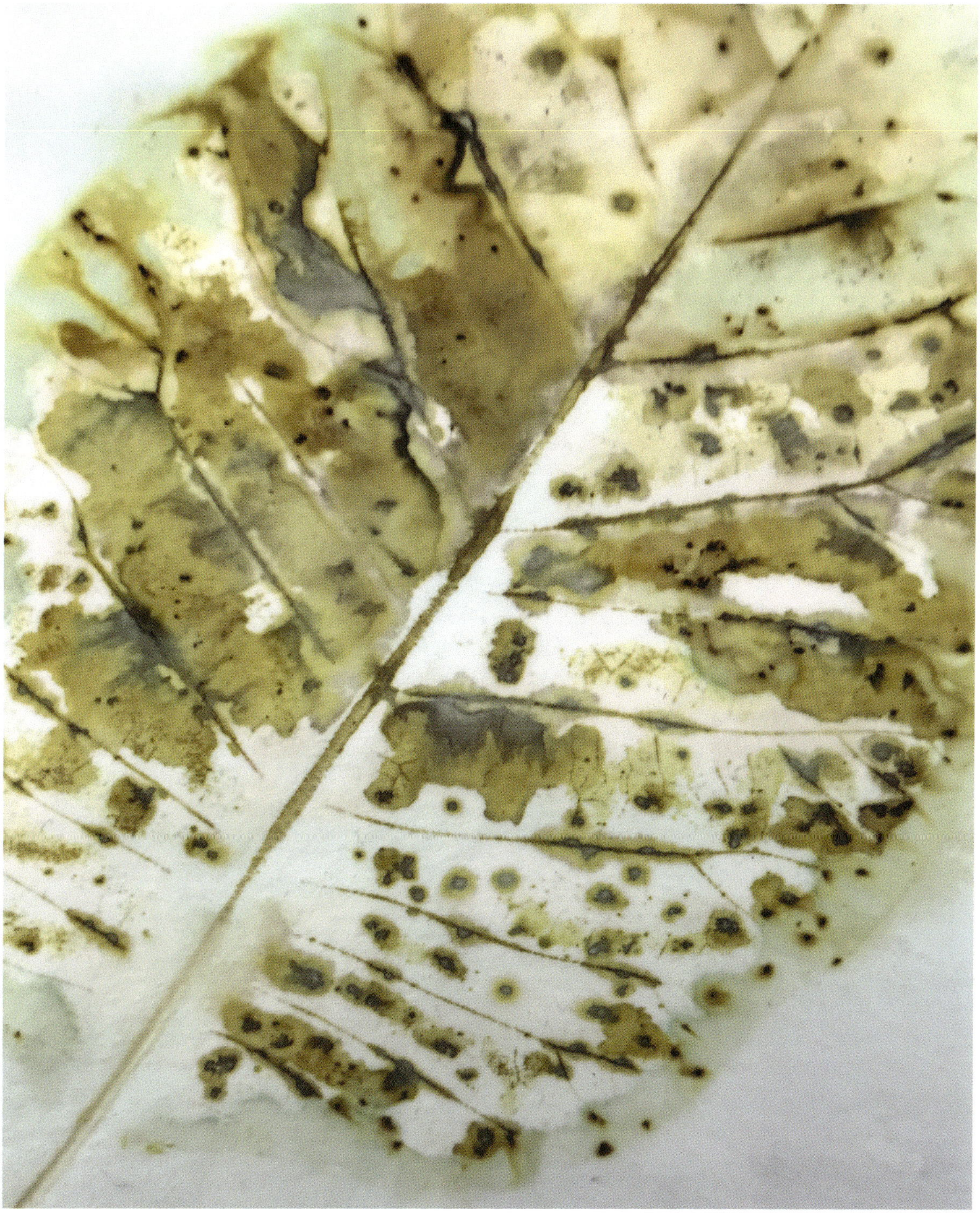

Hydrangea leaf botanically-dyed on paper.

MOVEMENT AGAIN

I suspect it is a restlessness in my nature that loves movement. I love to walk, and I love to dance in my studio when no one is watching. I love paths in gardens because they show a way to move forward. Sometimes the reveries on my walks are the most inspirational. My mind wanders along with my feet.

Back in the studio, I'm finally playing with black and white in the form of India ink. The ink seems to wander, too, capturing my mood and thoughts as it goes. I bought some A4 Moleskin watercolor books and each morning I let the ink run across the page using different tools. I love these pieces.

Of course, my mind says, "Don't you want to add some lush neutrals–something?" Hmmm, I guess not. For right now, I like the black and white and the sense of movement.

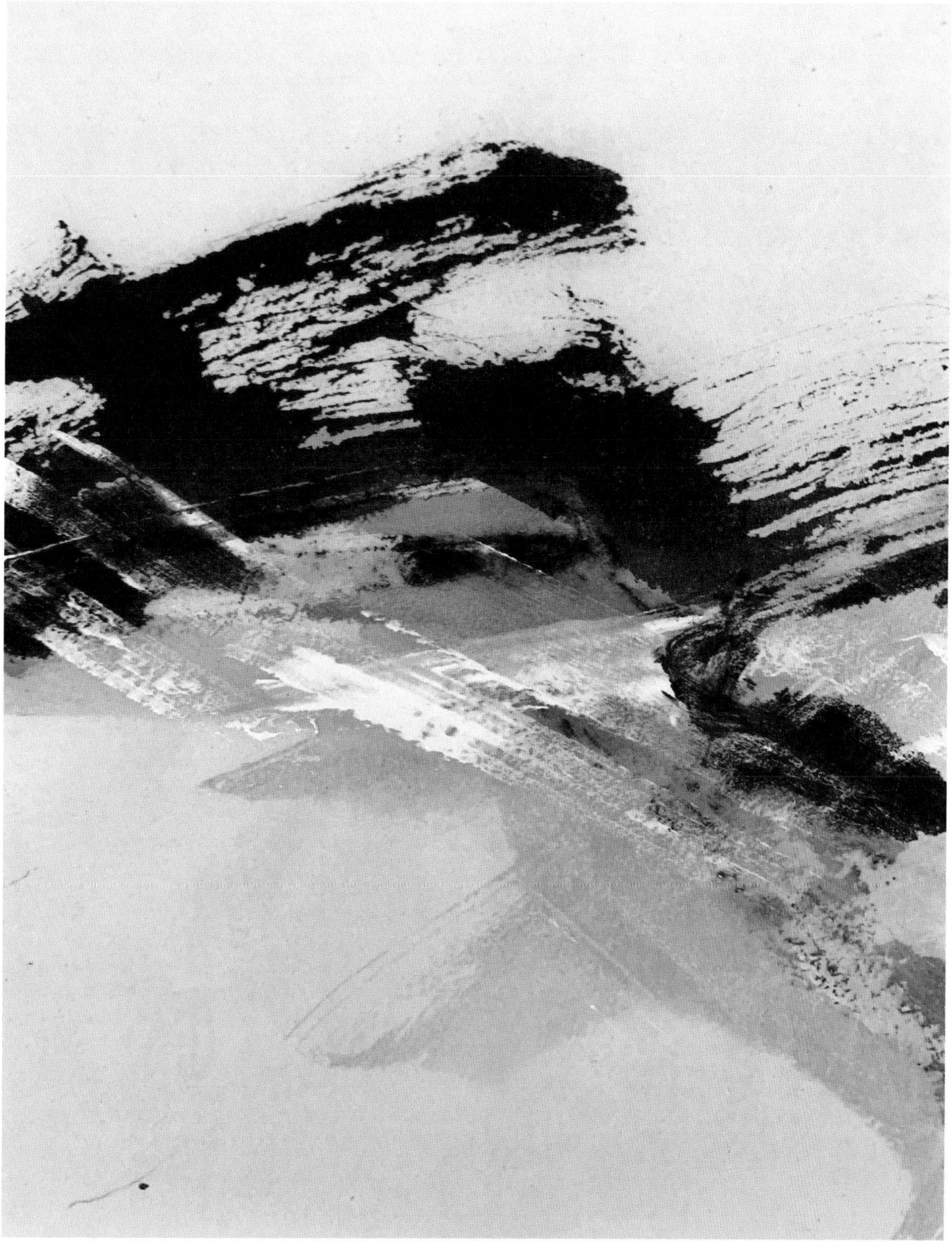

Movement
India ink and acrylic paint on washi paper, 7" × 9" (18cm × 23cm)

FLOW

I love it when a piece comes together easily and effortlessly and matches an inner image perfectly. My fingers tingle, and I know that I am in the flow and making a piece that I will love.

That doesn't always happen, however. Sometimes after spending hours making French knots, I decide they don't belong. It hurts as I cut them out. I know I was right to do it, though, when I feel a whoosh of relief that they are gone.

I learn more from these pieces than I do from the ones that just flow out of me.

I am forced to ask myself, "Is this me or some idea of what you think is right, Roberta?"

With art, it's relatively easy to ask these questions and make the changes. Often only a few hours are lost.

In life, though, making the necessary changes can be harder. There have been some periods in my life when everything was flowing and felt perfect. At other times, it is all a grind, and joy is gone.

It's hard to know what needs to shift or even if it does need to shift in those times. It's harder to trust that cutting out the French knots in our lives—relationships, jobs, houses—is necessary.

But just like with my art, I know I've made the right shift when I feel a whoosh of relief, and joy starts creeping back in.

TIME

It's good to remember that most of the famous artists we admire today were out of sync with their time, creating something that came so strongly from within that the rest of the world wasn't yet ready for. I think about Agnes Martin, for example; a Canadian-born American abstract painter. I remember first seeing her work in a New York gallery in 1986 and thinking, "This is art?" But those images hung in my memory for decades. Her pieces follow very few "rules," yet they are powerful and meditative and seem to come from the very fabric of life.

So many times I have been disappointed by a piece I just finished, only to find years later that I like it again. Conversely, sometimes I love a piece when I first finish it and then years later, I am not so enchanted.

I like to finish things—a plus for bank consulting, housework, and daily chores, yet not so good for art. I often have to leave a piece for months at a time to see what the next step should be. It doesn't want to be rushed.

Some artists are able to conceive the entire piece before they begin. That was true for me when I worked on the North Dakota ceramic pieces. I knew what they were to be ahead of time. But I've always thought my dad was there helping me make those pieces.

Usually, I have an intuitive feel for what I want the piece to be, but I have to find my way through the fog to get to the point when I know I got it right. My hands know more than my head.

Perhaps this is why artists are sometimes considered flaky or irresponsible. Honoring the process and the time that a piece deserves is tricky in the "real world" of schedules and deadlines. A new life is trying to come into being, and it is still frail. As an artist, my responsibility is to guard that new young life, not the deadline.

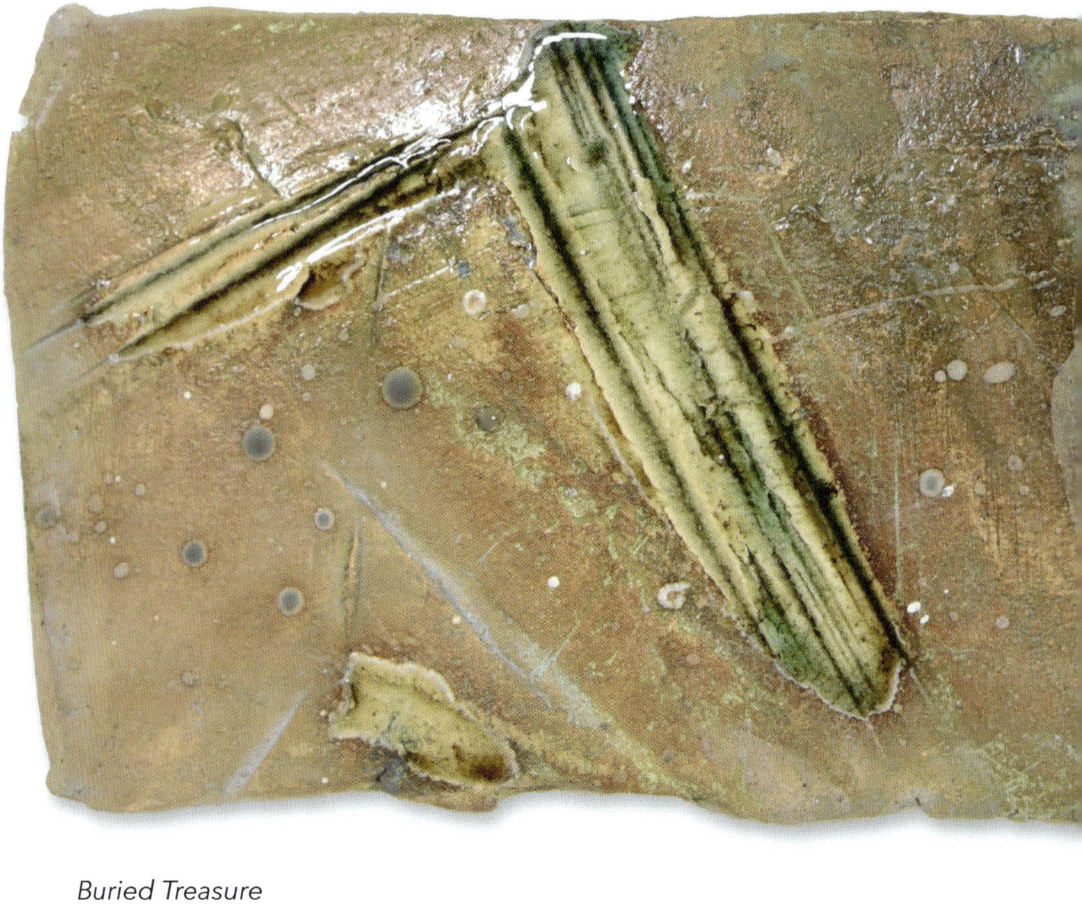

Buried Treasure
Stoneware 19" x 6" (48cm x 15cm)

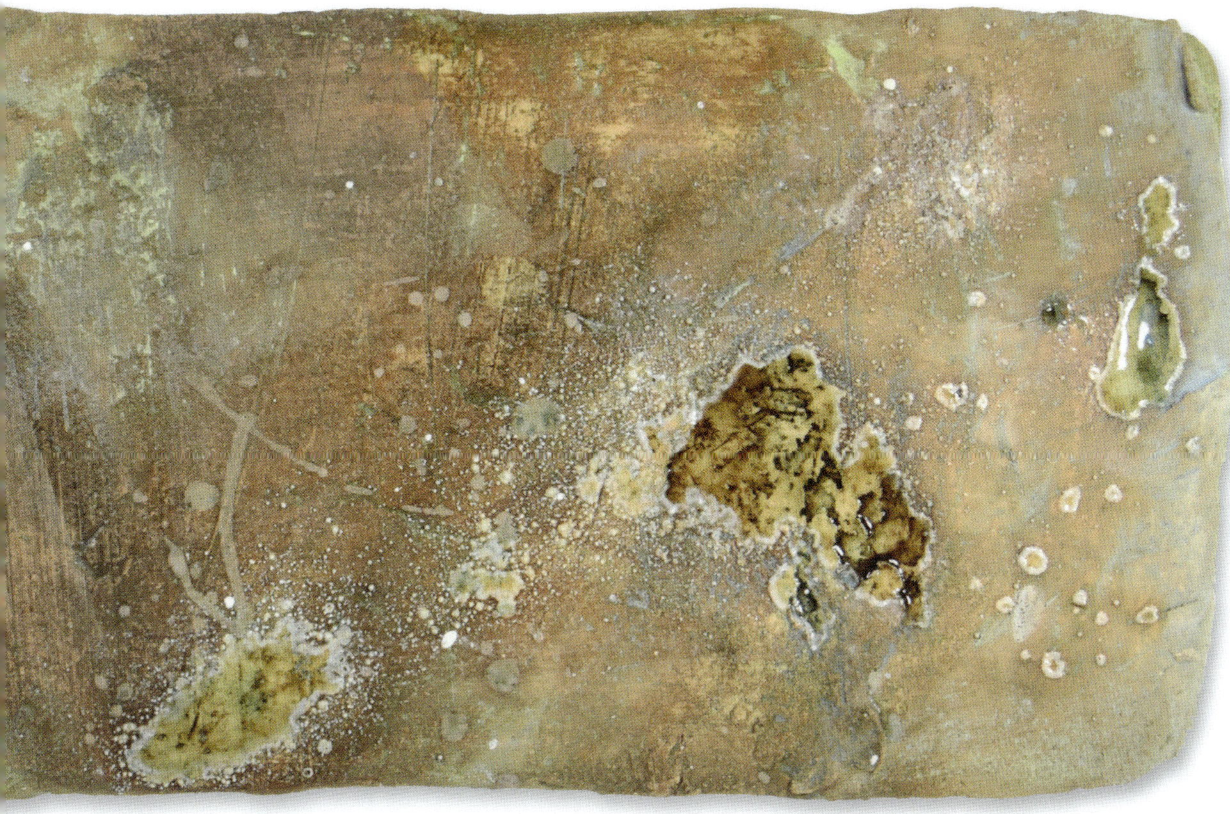

THE DIVINE

I stand in front of the blank sheet of beautiful Japanese washi paper, brush in hand. Sumi ink and green-gold and brown ochre watercolors have been watered down to a consistency I like. White acrylic paint is at the ready.

I breathe long and deep. I close my eyes. I clear my mind of expectations and plans.

When I open my eyes, my body takes over and, before I know it, my hand is moving across the paper with the Sumi ink. Ah—I am delighted. I love the mark it made.

It wants more, and I see my hand bravely adding the brown ochre. Before I can catch my breath, a dash of white has been added.

Fortunately, I stop. I close my eyes and breathe long and deep. I clear my mind and, when I open my eyes, I love what I see.

On my best days, I stop at the right moment. To me, it feels complete. It breathes. It has movement.

On other days, I let my critical eye and mind take over. Before I have time to stop and breathe, my mind says, "It's too simple; it needs more." I add and add until the painting has become a complicated mess.

On those days, perhaps I am learning the most important thing. I am learning to feel that subtle difference between when it is my mind and when it is the divine in motion.

In the rush of my other life, my outer life, it's always helpful to stop, breathe long and deep, clear my mind and notice the feeling. Am I using my rational, analytical, critical mind, or am I allowing the intuitive, the divine, to come into this part of my life as well?

On this day, I found my way.

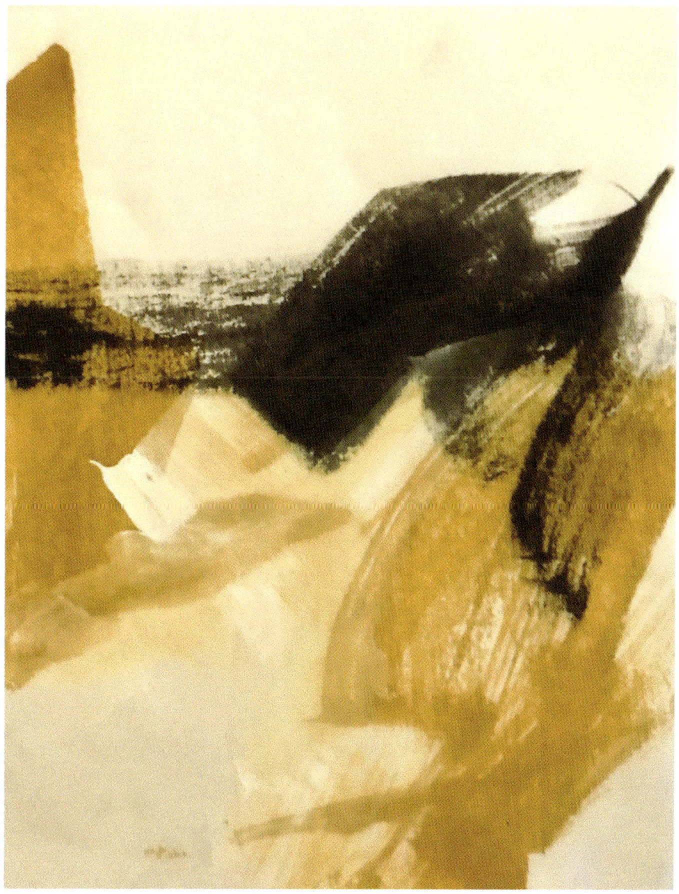

The Divine
Ink and water media on washi paper; 8" × 11" (20cm × 28cm)

DISCIPLINE

I think there are at least two types of discipline. One is the crack-the-whip kind that keeps us doing what we hate to do but is needed to get the job done. Another type is having the discipline to stick with what we love.

I love making art. I love writing. I love practicing yoga and walking; both help me with art and writing and life. And yet there's this little imp in me that says, "Oh, just lie on the couch for a while and relax."

If I resist that first urge toward the couch and start doing what I love, I can't pull myself away from it.

What is it that makes that darn couch keep calling? Or my task list keep nagging at me?

Maybe it doesn't matter. My job is to have the discipline to do what I love.

INNER AND OUTER WORLDS

I love looking at my calendar and seeing a week free of appointments; a week when I can hunker down and be alone with my thoughts.

I've learned it's easy to get lost in that, though. Years ago, when Bruce and I were living in Virginia, I was so tired of the outer world and so tired of bank consulting that I dreamed of a life as a full-time artist. I let that dream become a reality while I was working on architectural ceramics.

Although I had appointments with galleries and clients and wrote articles for a national clay magazine that required interviews with other ceramic artists, I was alone–with Bruce–and with uncluttered calendars.

I was too alone, though, and tried too hard to make art. I was no longer playing, I was working.

My work got stale, and I was frustrated.

When we later moved to Gig Harbor, Washington, from Virginia, I went in a completely opposite direction: from quiet, unscheduled days into the world of real estate. Oh, my gosh! My days were filled with constant interruptions as clients needed this or that. Also, "time is of the essence" is in most real estate transactions, so there is no opportunity to delay.

I learned so much from real estate: I learned about houses, marketing, client service, and the Gig Harbor community. And I made lots of friends. It was almost the complete opposite of my quiet artist life in Virginia, balancing out those years of solitude.

However, I made almost no art during those years.

It wore me out. And when the Great Recession of 2007 hit, I went back to bank consulting. Real estate had changed me, and I found I loved bank consulting again. I love my bank clients. Unlike real estate, I can better control my calendar, and it allows for quiet time. It gives me a better balance between inner and outer worlds. But it would not have been possible without my years in real estate.

I learned that I need to keep some kind of balance between my inner and outer worlds.

MAKERS

Lately, many artists have started calling themselves "makers." I kind of like that. It doesn't carry all the heavy connotations of calling yourself an artist.

And there is something about "making" that almost anyone can relate to. You make an ad campaign for your business. You make a wonderful meal that has creativity, thought, and love rolled up in it. You make a garden that moves you to a quiet, inner place. You sew a dress, knit a sweater, or devise a new strategy for your business. In a way, all of these things are art to me, made by "makers."

Why do I still call myself an artist then? Perhaps habit. Perhaps because I strive, whether or not I succeed, to create something that has the ability to transport me, and perhaps the viewer, to that aesthetic experience that is in the realm of the eternal, the mystical.

Either label is OK with me.

PATIENCE

More often than not, I turn to hand stitching in my work. It is so slow. When working with clay or paint, I'd swish this or that, and the gesture, the movement was the important thing. Not with hand stitch, however. It's slow. It takes time, and, in the slowness, the piece changes and requires adjustments.

Do you hear the impatience that is such a part of my nature? Oh, it's there.

Slow stitch requires slow time. So often all the tasks of daily living and working spring from urgency, and I sometimes bring that urgency to the studio. The stitch work is different then.

A few autumns ago, Bruce and I drove from Washington state to Minnesota to visit my sister Kate and her husband, John, at their lake cabin. They had an Ekornes recliner sitting in the corner of their cozy cabin that looked out on the lake and the fall trees. I glommed onto that chair, and, for at least five days, I had that chair and a slow routine of conversations, walks, easy food preparation with Kate, and stitch. Time slowed.

I brought several pieces with me to stitch, and I got lost each day in the quiet, meditative act of making those pieces. I played with them and had fun trying some things that worked and some that didn't.

On the drive there and back, 2,700 miles of mostly wide-open spaces and empty roads allowed for deeper conversations and gentle days with Bruce. As we drove along, we saw images of straw-colored fields edged with the reds, oranges, purples, and shocking yellows of wildflowers and grasses; the soft gray of sages; and dark green firs studded in between. I hope the images will stay with me for a lifetime.

That slow time quieted my mind and allowed me to slow stitch with joy.

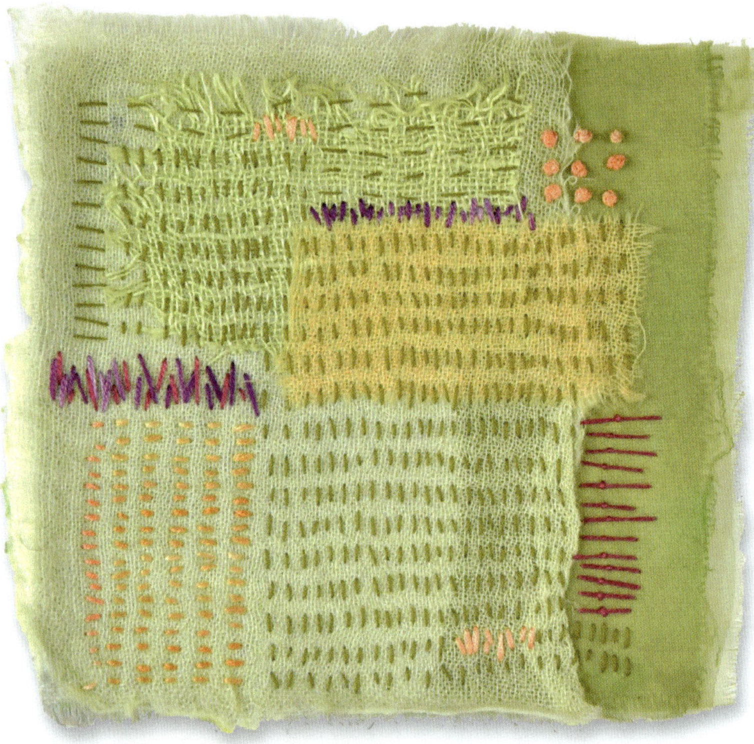

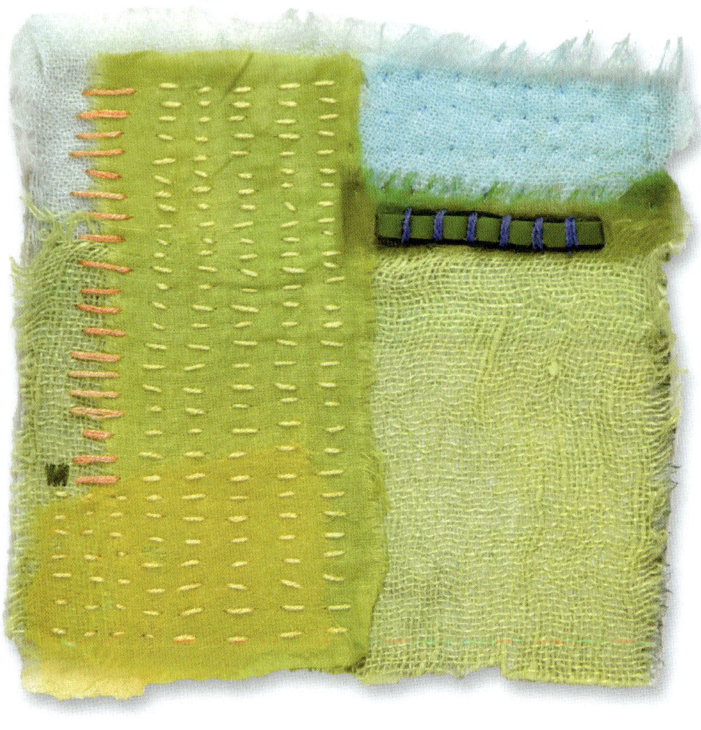

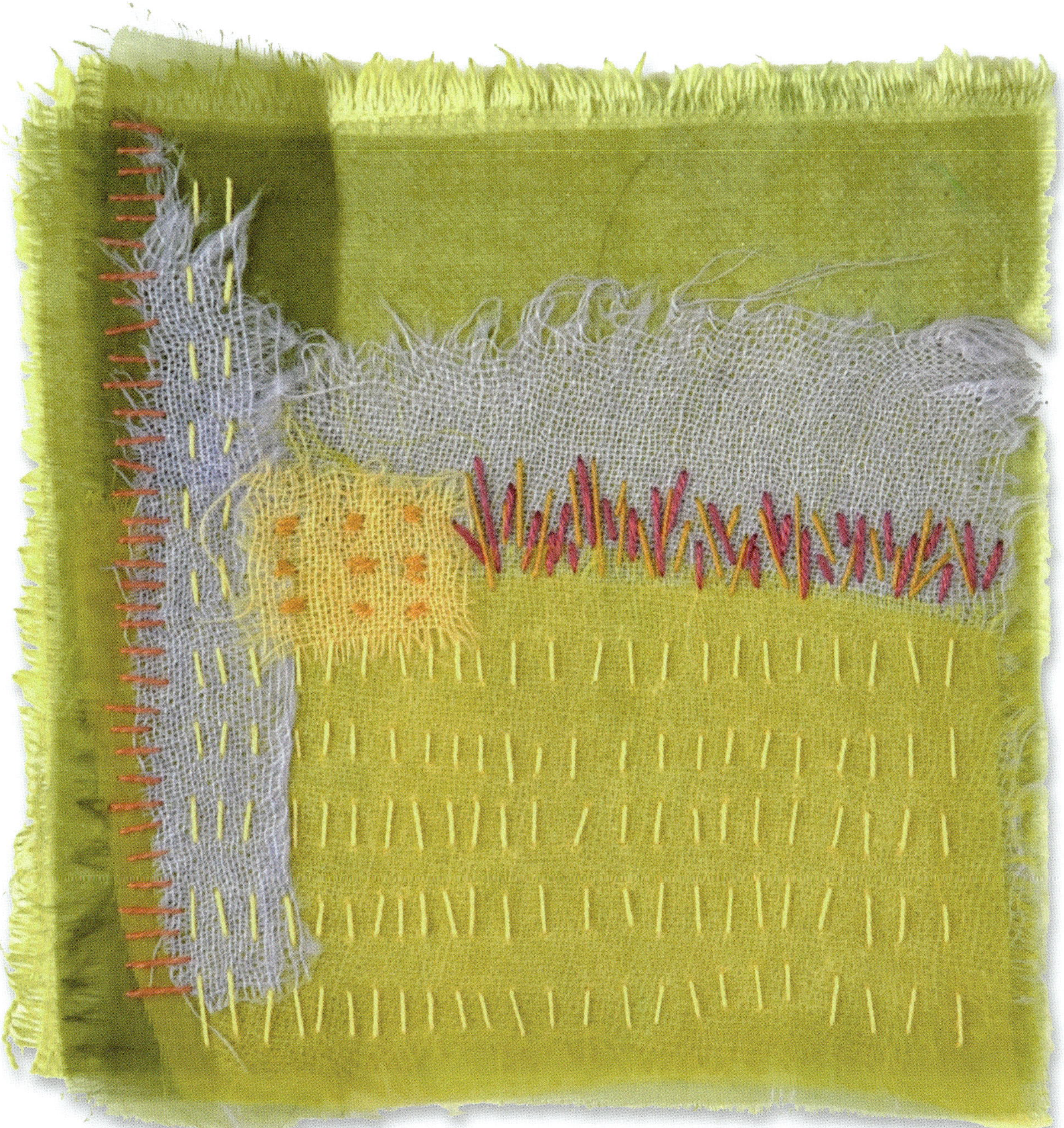

Minnesota Lake Time
Silks, linens, and canvas with stitch, 5" × 5" (13cm × 13cm)

GROUND COVERS

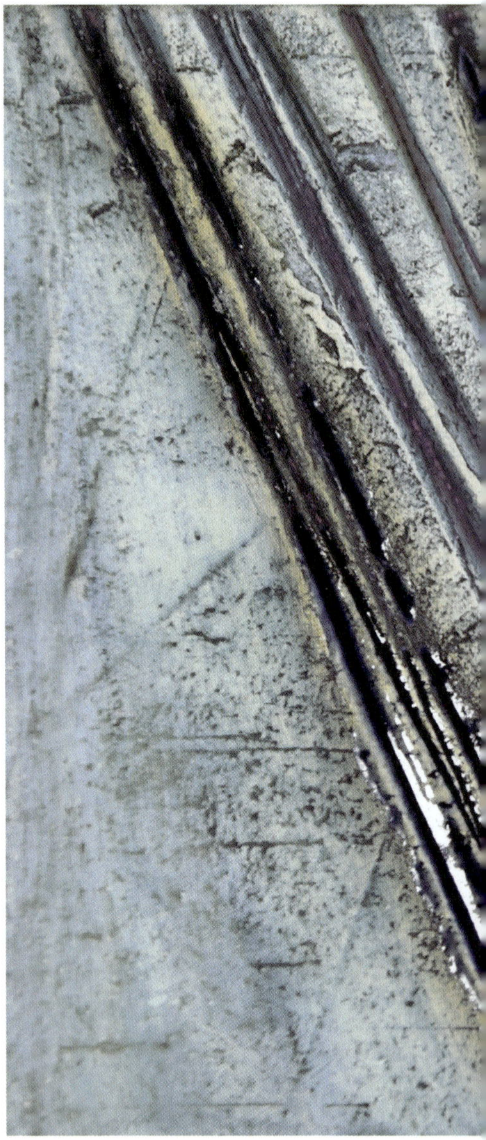

The many parts of anything moving together in harmony will always fill me up and make my heart sing. I see it in my garden. I see it in my love for quilts and mosaics.

It started early. One day when I was about ten years old, I was riding with my dad, heading toward the Minneapolis-Saint Paul airport, where there are lots of overpasses and exchanges. Normally, traffic like that made me nervous but not that day. The cars seemed to move in a perfectly orchestrated symphony and brought me to what I now understand was a mystical experience. The beauty of their choreographed movements must have rung a bell in my own very young character.

In my garden, varieties of sedum mix with purple ajuga and form a magical carpet as they blend and make room for each other. A foxglove or Welsh poppy will find a little patch to fit itself in.

I want to have space in my life for so many things: family, art, gardens, friends, walking, yoga, cooking, work. I try to set schedules. I think to myself: I will write from five to seven in the morning, walk from seven to eight, do bank work from eight to noon, have time in the studio in the afternoon, grab a half hour in the garden, cook in the late afternoon . . . and on it goes; a recipe for disaster because I can never segregate the pulls on my time that way. It's exhausting, and the joy goes out of everything.

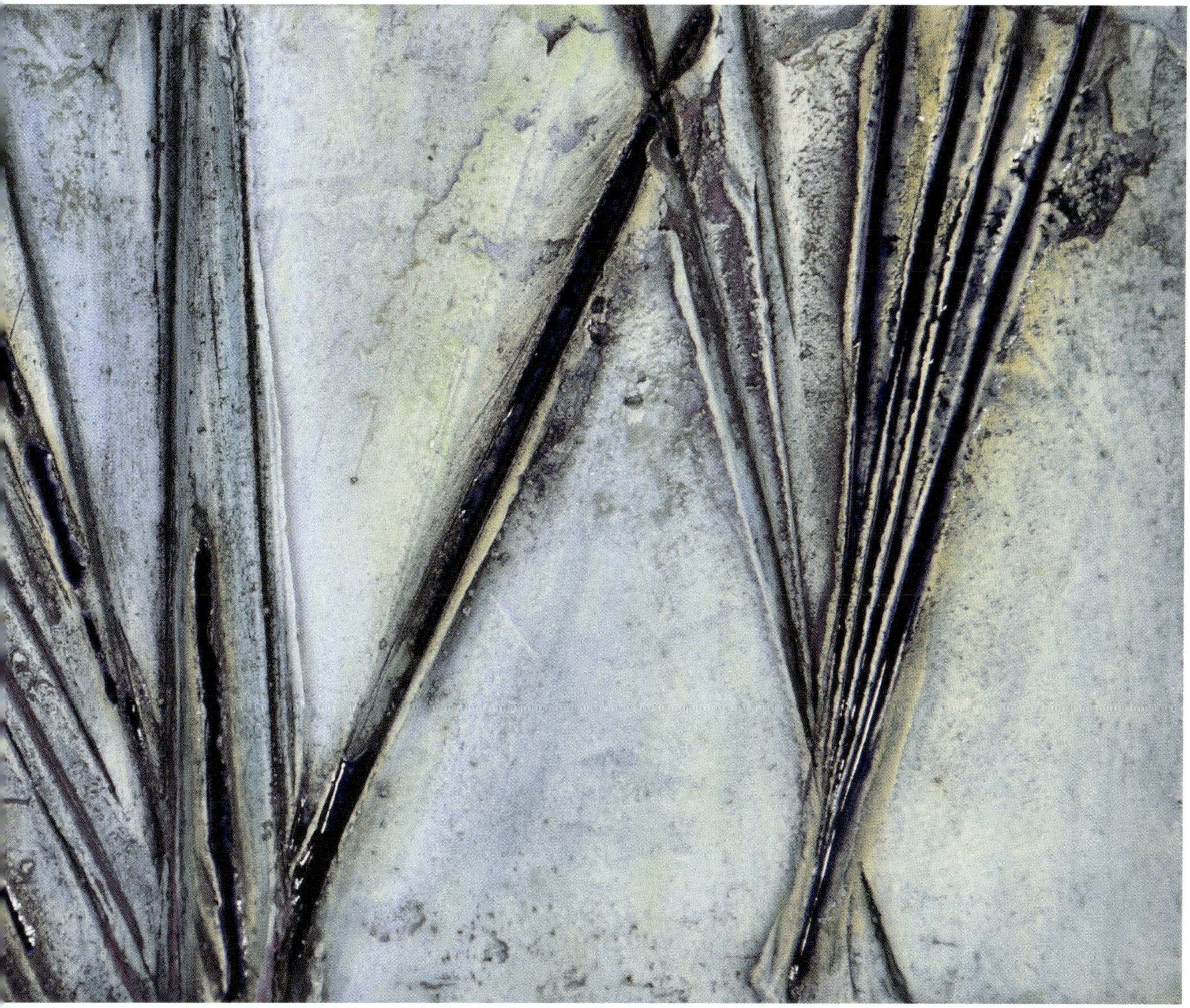

Gemstone II
Stoneware tile, 12″ x 7½″ (30cm x 19cm)

The ground covers remind me that I need to let the many parts of myself move together effortlessly, beautifully, like those cars on the Minnesota freeway. There are days now when I move with my heart: writing some, walking some, practicing yoga, pulling a few weeds, and thinking about art and clients and Bruce. I still wish I could set a schedule, but I am wiser now and try to let the intuition move me about.

PAUSE

One month recently, the garden had me and wouldn't let me go. I am enthralled with her beauty now and know that it is the best garden I've ever had. It is full of so many plants that I love: Japanese maples, peonies, daffodils, lilies, clematis, hellebores, Epimedium, and hydrangeas. There are paths and places to sit, and I actually sit in them, sucking up the beauty around me.

Almost no painting or stitch work was done during that month. I wrote very little. Ideas would flit across my mind, lingering to give me time to catch them. Even when I did pause long enough to notice them, I let them go. I was busy.

This happens in life. However, now that sanity has returned and the garden has released me, I am painting again. I lost momentum, though. I am writing again, but it feels stiffer. It will take time to re-enter that creative flow that keeps me moving deeper into me.

Oh, well. The garden was worth it.

STARDUST

Oh, the night sky . . . I wish I could be out in the desert on a clear night and see the full magnificence of it.

The stars always remind me of those who have gone before: my mom, who always supported my artwork and loved me; my dad, with his wisdom and humor; Ila, who prompted me to change; my friend Kathy Eyer, who struggled with and lost a battle with depression; my friend Eileen Bitney, who died way too young from Lupus; Vally, of course . . . and so many others.

I like to think that a bit of stardust falls down on me and touches me with these loved ones who have gone before me.

We lose so much not being able to see that night sky in all its splendor. Our own city lights can beguile, but they don't have the majesty and the wisdom of the stars.

We need—I need—to bring the awe of the night sky back into sight.

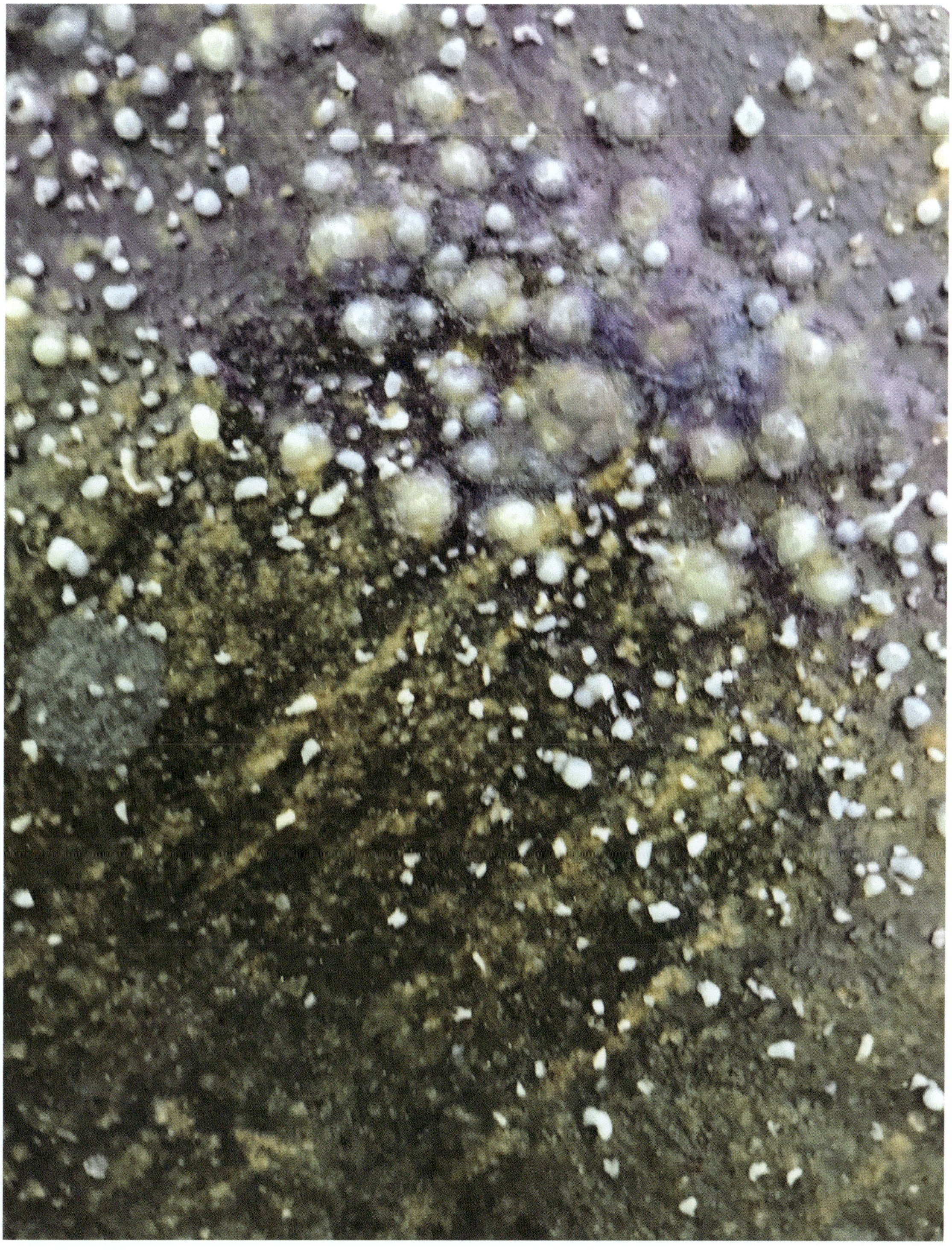

Close-up of ceramic glaze

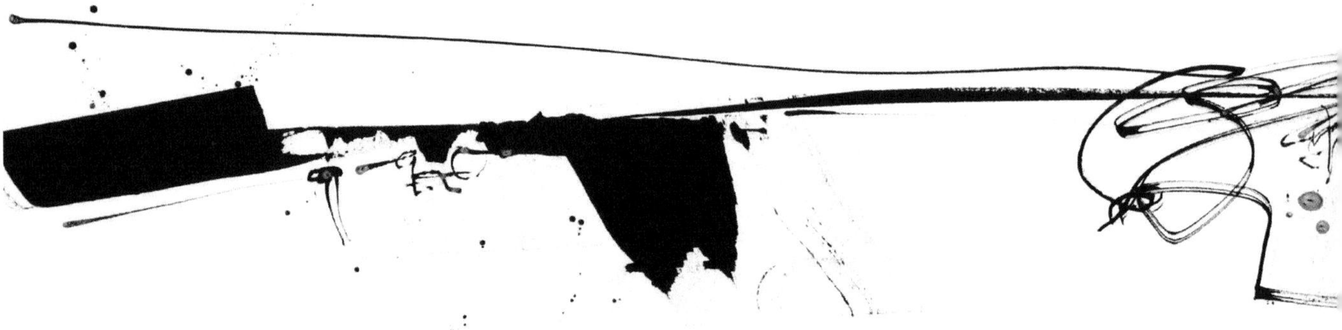

Moving
India ink on Arches paper, 11" × 30" (28cm ×76cm)

THE LONG WALK

Parkinson's Disease • Play • Salvation • Hospice • Grief • The New Reality • Beginning Again • Today • And Finally

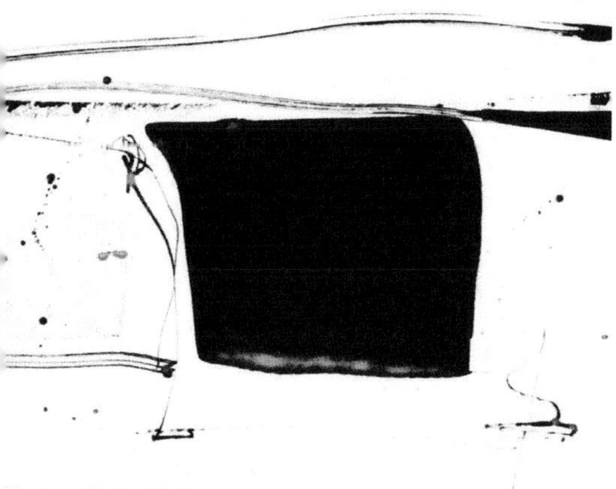

PARKINSON'S DISEASE

I suspect that it was many years before Bruce was actually diagnosed with Parkinson's that it began to take its toll.

Eventually I became a full-time caregiver. To all the other caregivers out there, I send my love and every bit of energy I can to you. Every caregiving role is different, and every disease or injury that requires it is different. And the relationship between the caregiver and the cared-for is different. All of them are challenging.

It felt so cruel to lose Bruce one day at time, that is, to see such a kind, loving man, the brilliant strategist, get confused. To see the man I love begin to have difficulty walking and needing so much help was heartbreaking. I know other caregivers in similar circumstances must feel the same.

Through each stage of the progression, I had to learn strategies to deal with the change. As a shift happened, I cried a lot. I became angry at times, and frustrated and full of grief. Then I would have to figure out how to adapt until the next progression occurred and more solutions were needed.

I learned that sometimes I needed to ask for help. I hated that. Sometimes I cried in public when I wished I didn't. I became more vulnerable, and it showed. I hated that, too. Those were probably good adaptations for me, but I hated them nonetheless.

Painted washi papers and stitch, 4" × 5" (10cm × 13cm)
I went down to the studio one day and my hands assembled small left-over pieces of paper. I loved the fragility of the papers that when bound together became strong. It felt like me.

Our life became centered at home, except for Bruce's physical therapy sessions. Going out for meals became increasingly difficult and travel was impossible; he wasn't interested anymore anyway. I hated to leave him, but I was still working at the time and it was necessary to have other caregivers come in on occasion.

Because of all of this staying put, we developed a quieter rhythm in our lives. We often just sat together on the couch in companionable silence. I once read, who knows where, that we are attracted to others partially by their smell. I always loved Bruce's smell and found comfort in it.

Like many caregivers, there developed a deep sorrow to my days; I found that it quieted by spending time in my studio.

I know that that studio time is what saved me; it kept joy and wonder and beauty in the forefront of my life.

PLAY

About then, the word "play" seemed to pop out of every book I read and every sign I saw. I've noticed this before. I think it's my intuition knocking me on the head to get my attention.

I love to plan out a body of artwork. I love to do it even though, time after time, I have to abandon the plan when I have just begun because I am bored with the work. It has lost its joy. Art does not like to be corralled.

Thankfully, Stuart Brown's important book *Play: How It Shapes the Brain*, Opens the Imagination, and Invigorates the Soul arrived in my Audible recommendations.

How is play different than doing what I like to do? According to Brown, play is purposeless and voluntary. We are not trying to accomplish anything. We have an inherent attraction to it, we forget about time and ourselves, and we always want more of it. It gives us energy and a whole host of other things that help us survive and thrive and stay young.

Clearly, I needed to bring more play into my studio.

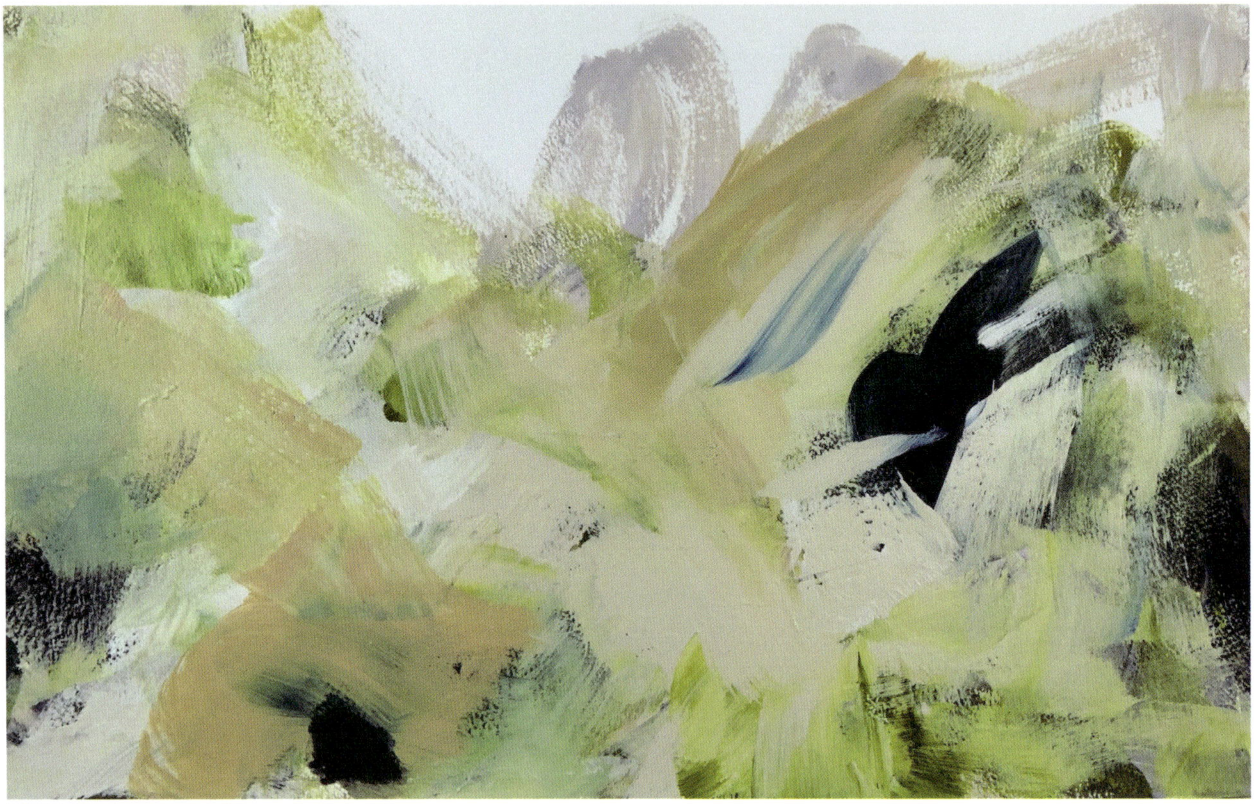

Spring
Acrylic on Arches paper, 22.5" × 15.5" (57cm × 39cm)

SALVATION

With the idea of play hovering, Nancy Hillis's book, *The Artist's Journey*, came through my Instagram feed right on cue. In a click of intuition, I bought the book. In a day, I read it. The next day I purchased the online course.

Thanks to her guidance, I began painting again—on paper, on Masonite, on washi paper with huge brushes, small pencils, oil sticks, charcoals, and pastels.

I was having fun again. I was curious, surprised, and energized. I was playing once again.

I had no idea where it would lead me, because I was going in a direction that wasn't controlled by me.

Would I keep using textiles? Would I keep doing collage? I wanted to, but it seemed to be out of my hands. What I consciously wanted my art to be seemed to dissipate when I had brush in hand and let my body and my hand dictate what came next.

In the ensuing months, I went through reams of old paper that had lain untouched for decades. And then I bought more. So many of the paintings were what Hillis calls "the paintings we view as ugly." She encourages us to welcome them, to see the parts of them that may be a harbinger of deeper work to come.

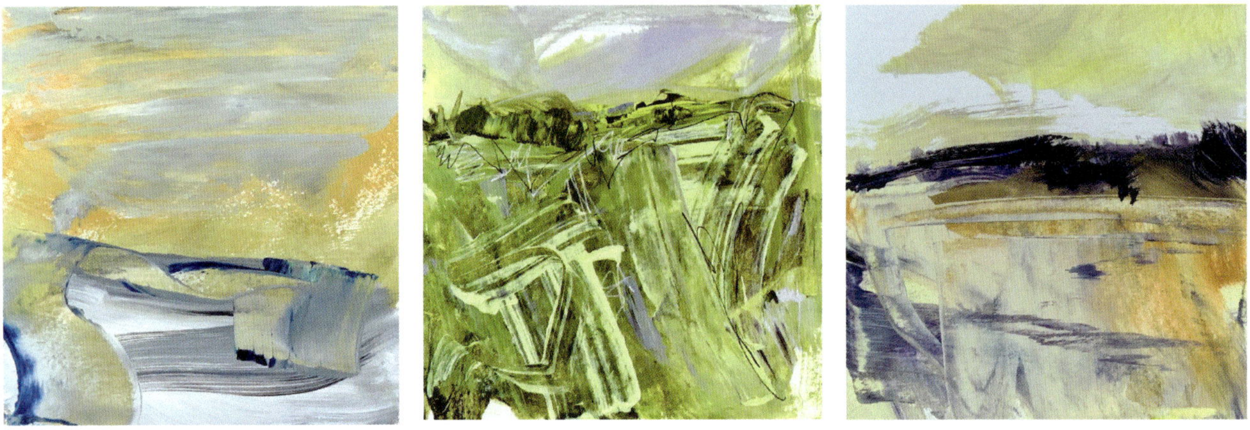

Small journal pages of abstracted landscapes while playing with paint and charcoal. 7" × 7" (18cm × 18cm)

Trust yourself to explore the things that scare you. These are the unexpressed, unexplored parts of yourself where your unlived dreams reside. This is the realm of play, improvisation, and pure creativity.[2]

I kept going. I kept trusting.

The acrylic paint felt plastic to me after all the years of clay's earthy feel and the soft caress of fabric and silk thread. But I kept going. I couldn't wait to get back in the studio again.

Each morning I brought my paintings up to show Bruce. We looked at them and laughed and loved and had something else to think about besides Parkinson's.

---

[2] *The Artist's Journey*, Nancy Hillis, MD, www.nancyhillis.com, page 61.

Then one day, in the same way that I was throwing paint on the paper or board, I began to wildly machine stitch on beautiful washi paper—the washi paper that always takes me back to Japan and that quiet, timeless aesthetic I so love.

After stitching, I found my hand applying ink and acrylic paint. I applied more and more and more paint and then more water. I let it dry and started to cut it up and put it back together with hand and machine stitching.

My grief leaked out. My love spilled out.

I knew that it was the deep sorrow that pushed me, compelled me, to find a way to play again. It demanded that I go deeper into my artwork. My artistic practice was deepening and changing again. It was saving me.

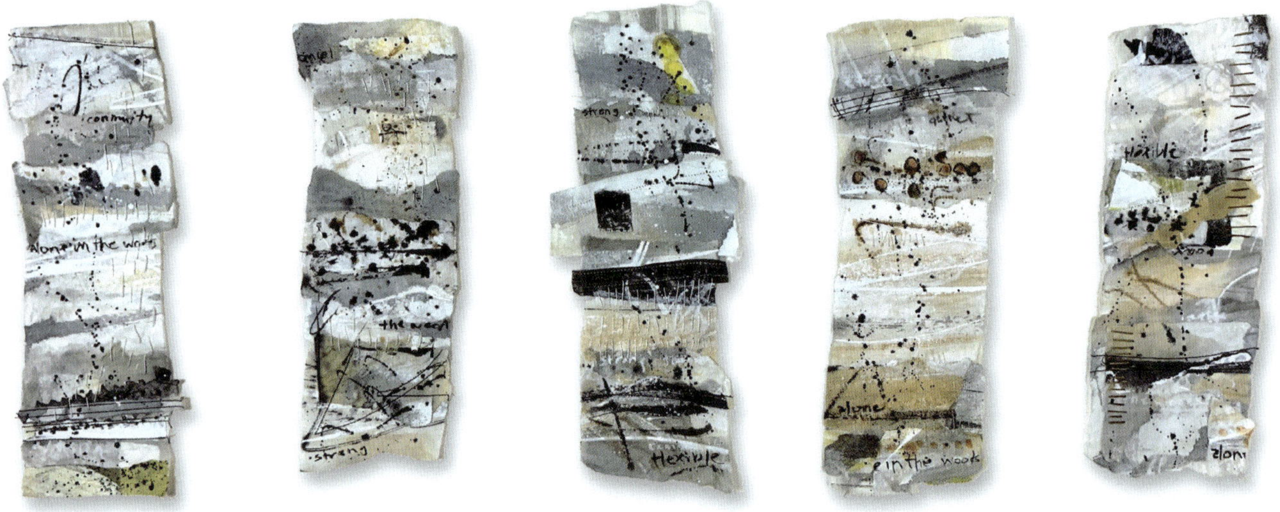

"In the Woods" Series
Each piece approximately 4.5" × 12.5" (11cm × 32cm)

HOSPICE

Bruce started hospice at our home. It happened so fast. One week he was walking, albeit slowly, and the next week he was bedridden.

For four weeks I cared for him, and we talked and laughed and cried and had precious moments together.

Then he slipped into a coma. It seemed he would pass quickly but then something changed, and he seemed to rest into the moment. On day five, I thought, "How will I ever go forward without him?" I started to think about what would save me without Bruce.

I knew my consulting work was important; it keeps me connected to the outside world. I knew that artwork would both distract and comfort me.

In the middle of that fifth night of coma, I realized that my current studio and office were dysfunctional for what I would need in the years ahead. I'm good at space planning and set about drafting room layouts. Three hours later I had it figured out. I could separate the painting and textile studios. I could move my office to a current storage room that looked out on a courtyard garden and would permit a better configuration than the current one.

On the morning of day six, I took Bruce's hand and told him my plans for rearranging the downstairs workspaces. His breathing changed, and within a few hours he passed away. Was he waiting for me to figure out how to go forward? I like to think so and that he approved of the plan.

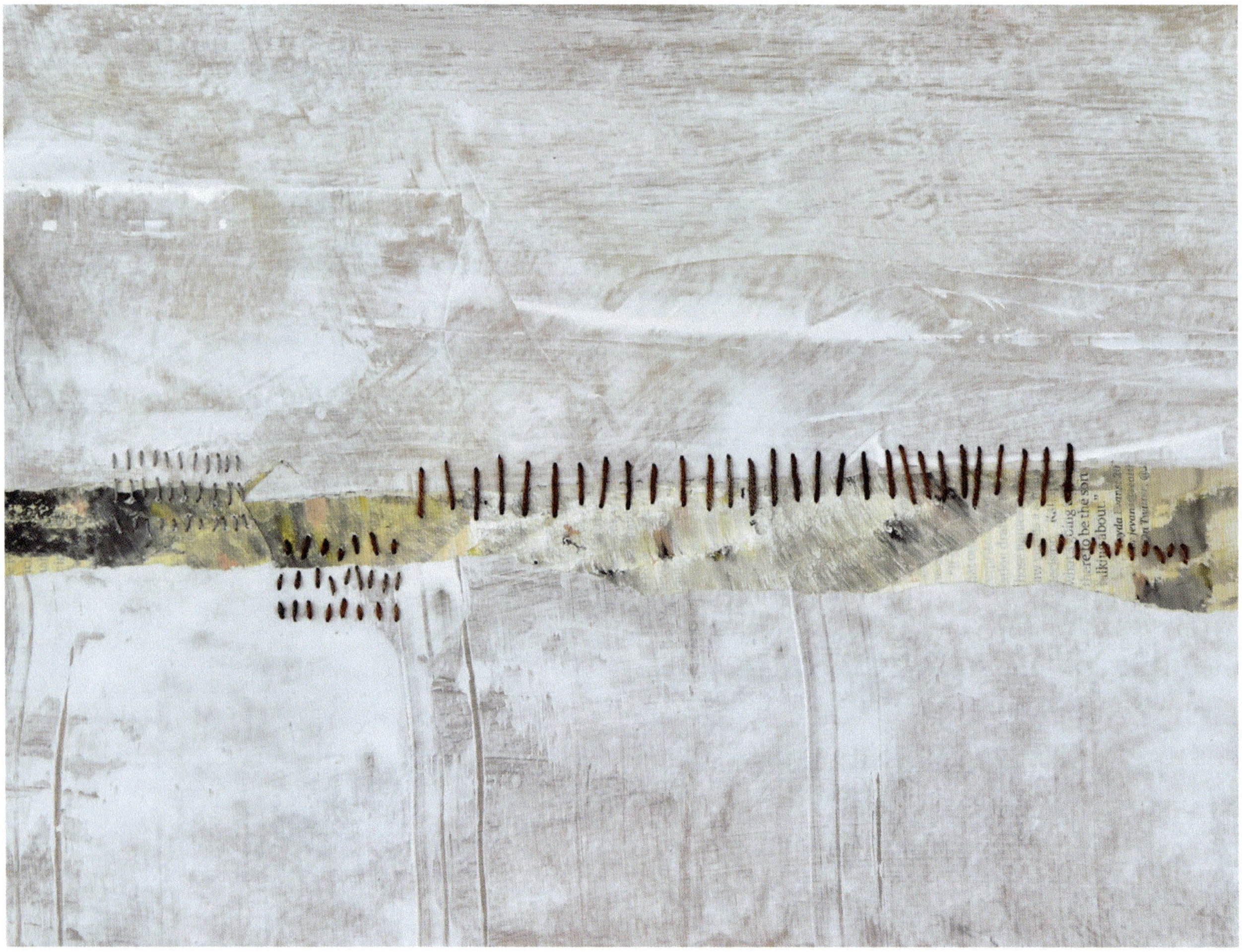

Winter Fields
Acrylic and stitch on cotton paper with collage, 11" x 9" (28cm x 23cm)

GRIEF

In the first month after his memorial service, I took on the Herculean task of moving my office and studios all around. It kept me distracted. And in the end, each space felt more conducive to what I thought I needed to accomplish.

But in month two, I didn't go down to either space. Instead, I sat on the couch, energy zapped, shocked when I realized that weeks had gone by without him. I suspect that grief releases chemicals that numb us so we can't feel the full impact of the new reality all at once. But the chemicals eventually wore off and my new reality was impossible to ignore.

Grief sneaks up on me. It's billowy and amorphous, like a cloud seeping into every moment, cloaking joy and the world around me.

I needed it. I didn't want to be out in the world. I wanted to be in our home, alone with memories of our times together. I wanted to know that he was OK. I wanted to feel him again. I didn't want to forget his smell, his touch, his kindness, and our ways together.

I couldn't move quickly. My inner and outer worlds were out of sync and needed to come into alignment again. Would they ever?

I thought that with less time spent caregiving, I would be able to spend more time in the studio and doing other things I love. Instead, I would become breathless when walking just a few yards. My heart would pound and keep me awake at night. My diet was terrible. I couldn't drag myself off the couch to fix something nutritious to eat. I didn't go for walks or practice yoga. I didn't go down to my studios.

I finally came to see that, for my own physical health, I would have to change. I found a good doctor and went to him with the goal of restoring my health.

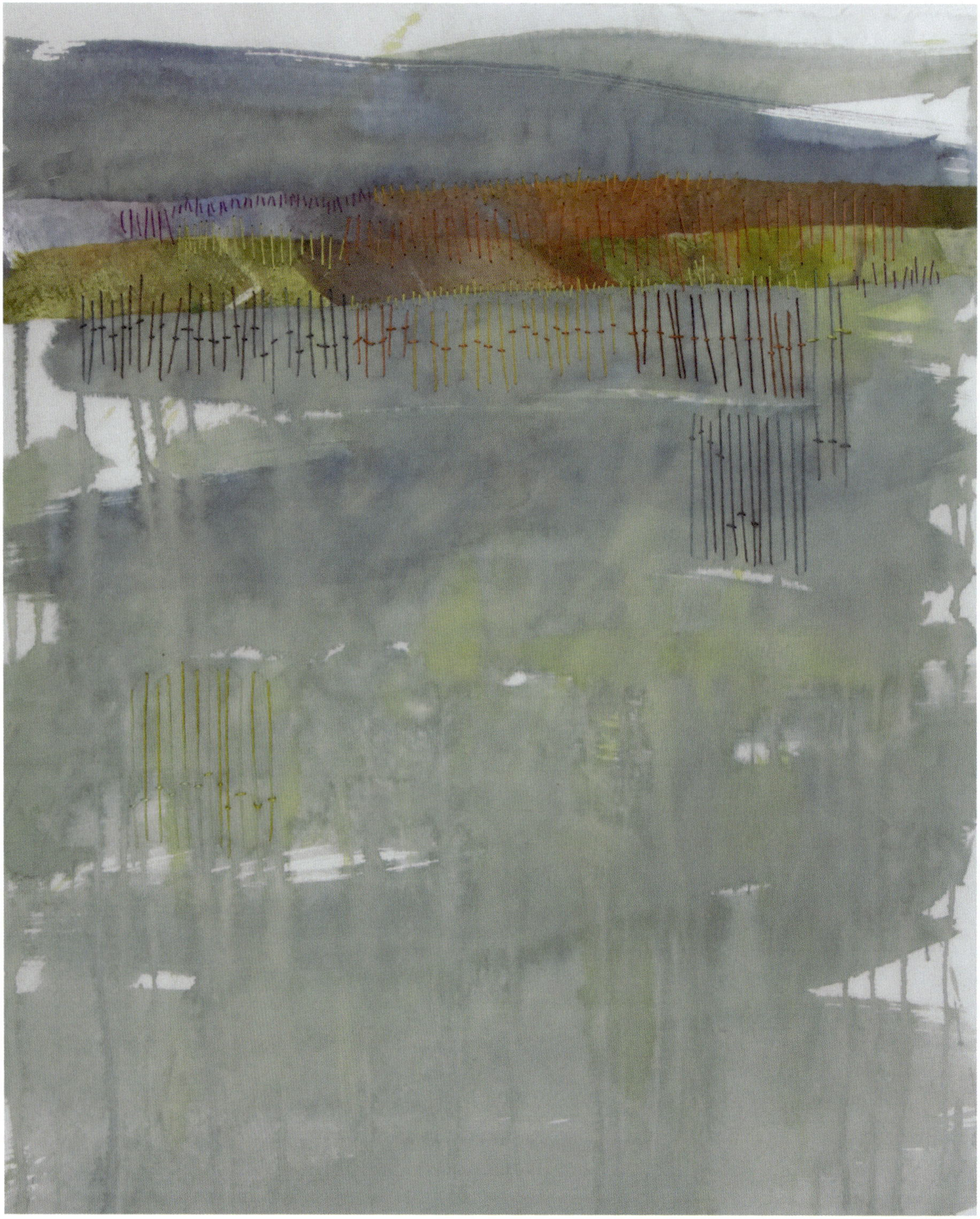

Rain
Washi paper with paint, collage, and stitch

THE NEW REALITY

It turned out that it wasn't all grief keeping me on the couch; my own health issues were brewing. In December of that year, I discovered I had severe, really severe, anemia and was immediately given two units of blood. Then the search began to find out why I was so severely anemic. More tests were needed. I hate medical tests, but I had to buck up and get them done.

Over the next three months, I had at least thirty blood draws, two bone marrow biopsies, two blood transfusions, CT and PET scans, a lymph node biopsy, and more. The easy things to fix anemia were quickly eliminated.

Waiting for a diagnosis was agonizing. I conjured up all sorts of horrors. I grieved for the loss of the future I thought I had. I scared myself. I sat on the couch and cried. I was so tired I could barely move.

Thankfully, friends and family stepped up to help. A friend who is a retired nurse went to doctor appointment after doctor appointment with me. My sister Kate checked in with me almost daily.

I missed Bruce every day, and although I'm glad he didn't have to watch me go through this, I also wished he was here. He was my person, my next of kin.

Finally, I got a diagnosis: a rare indolent B cell lymphoma in my bone marrow and a lot of lymph nodes. Stage four. I learned more than I ever wanted to know about blood cancers. Still, the good news was that it is treatable.

I read about survival rates and chemotherapy treatments. I joined a Facebook lymphoma support group and read about the horrors of the different treatment regimens.

I listened for my next step.

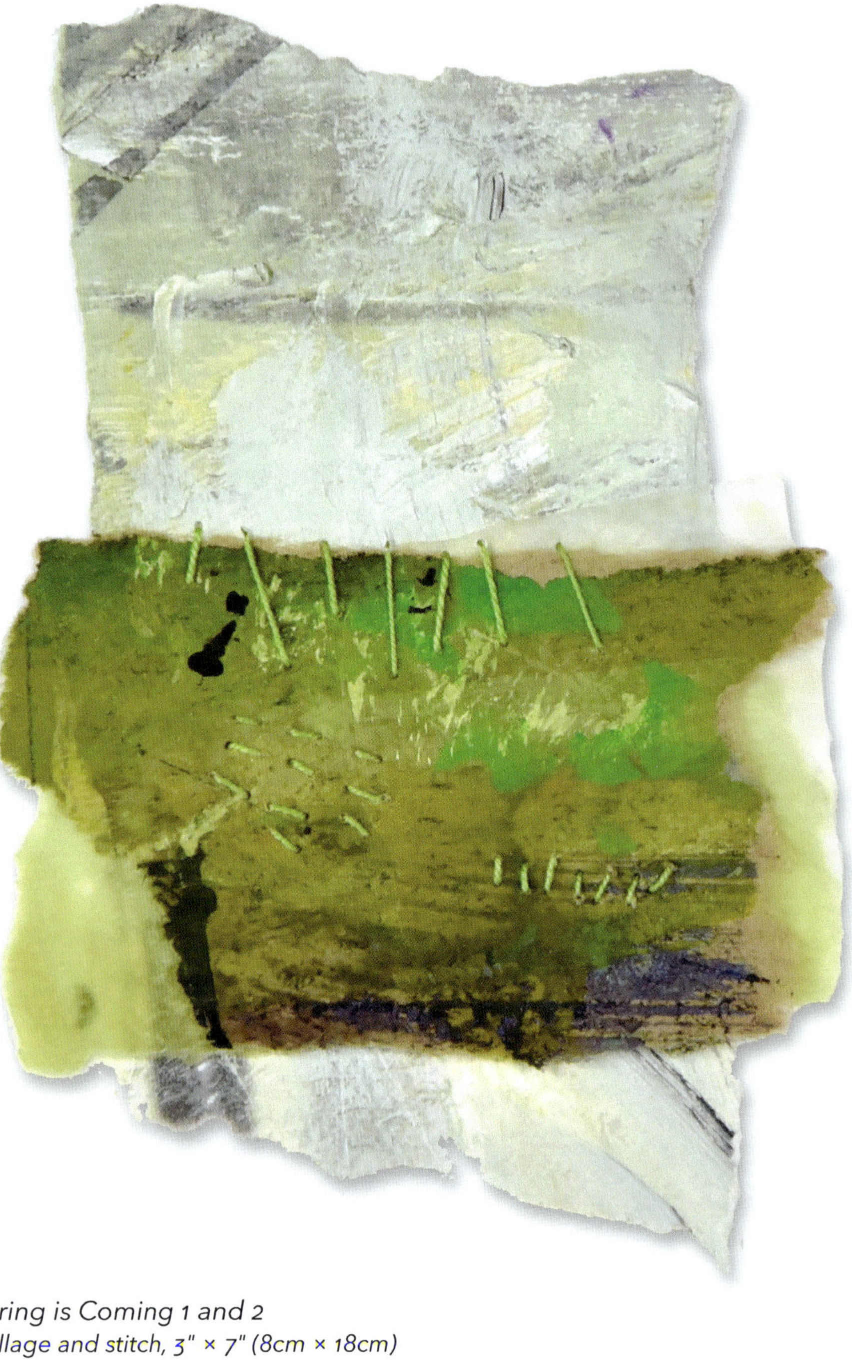

Spring is Coming 1 and 2
Collage and stitch, 3" × 7" (8cm × 18cm)
I can manage making small pieces. They distract me. I get lost in them.

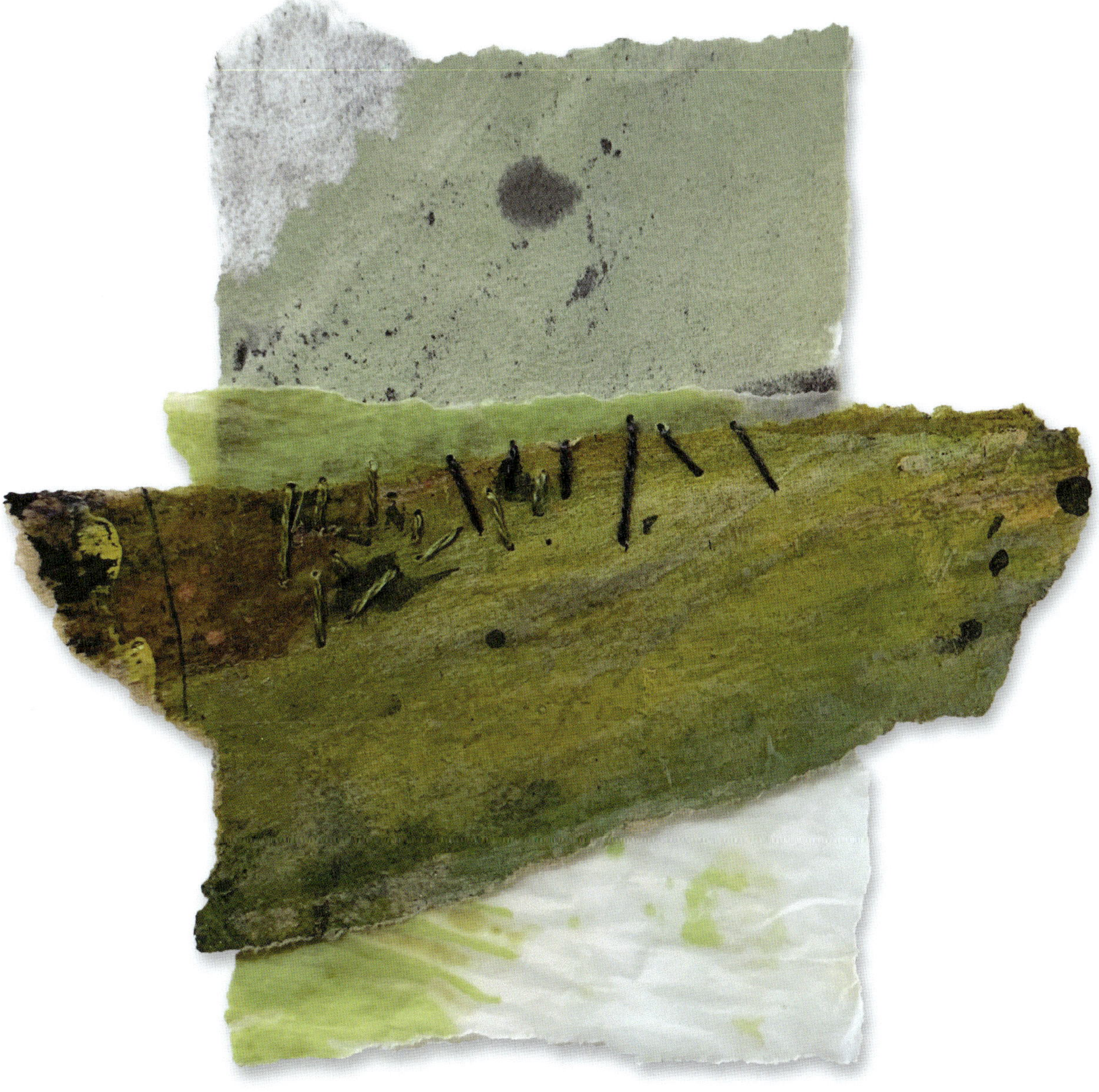

BEGINNING AGAIN

Three months after that first blood transfusion, I began chemotherapy. After a very rough start with severe allergic reactions to the first treatment regimen, I was able to tolerate a second treatment regimen. I got better, and my anemia was gone. However, I still had many more months of chemotherapy and tests to make sure that the lymphoma really had gone into remission. But I was on the way.

I began to think about the year ahead of me and the years after that. What do I want to have in my life in the coming year besides cancer and the fatigue that comes with chemotherapy?

And then it hit me: small pieces.

I went down to the freshly arranged textile studio, and my hands start putting paper together into pieces that remind me of the tidelands outside my window. The small pieces come together quickly.

They became a series I call "Summer on the Water." In a series, they gain strength; one seems to inform the other. I am excited about the direction and know I'll be able to make them even if fatigued from lymphoma and chemotherapy.

I loved the re-organization in the textile studio. The painting studio feels so open and functional. My office allows more efficiency.

I was right: making the changes in the downstairs rooms helped me find the way forward in the year after Bruce passed. I thought I needed to do that for life without Bruce, but, as it turned out, I also needed them to get through my own health issues.

My old enthusiasm lingers just below the surface, and I begin to catch glimmers of it. I walk around the garden and enjoy seeing

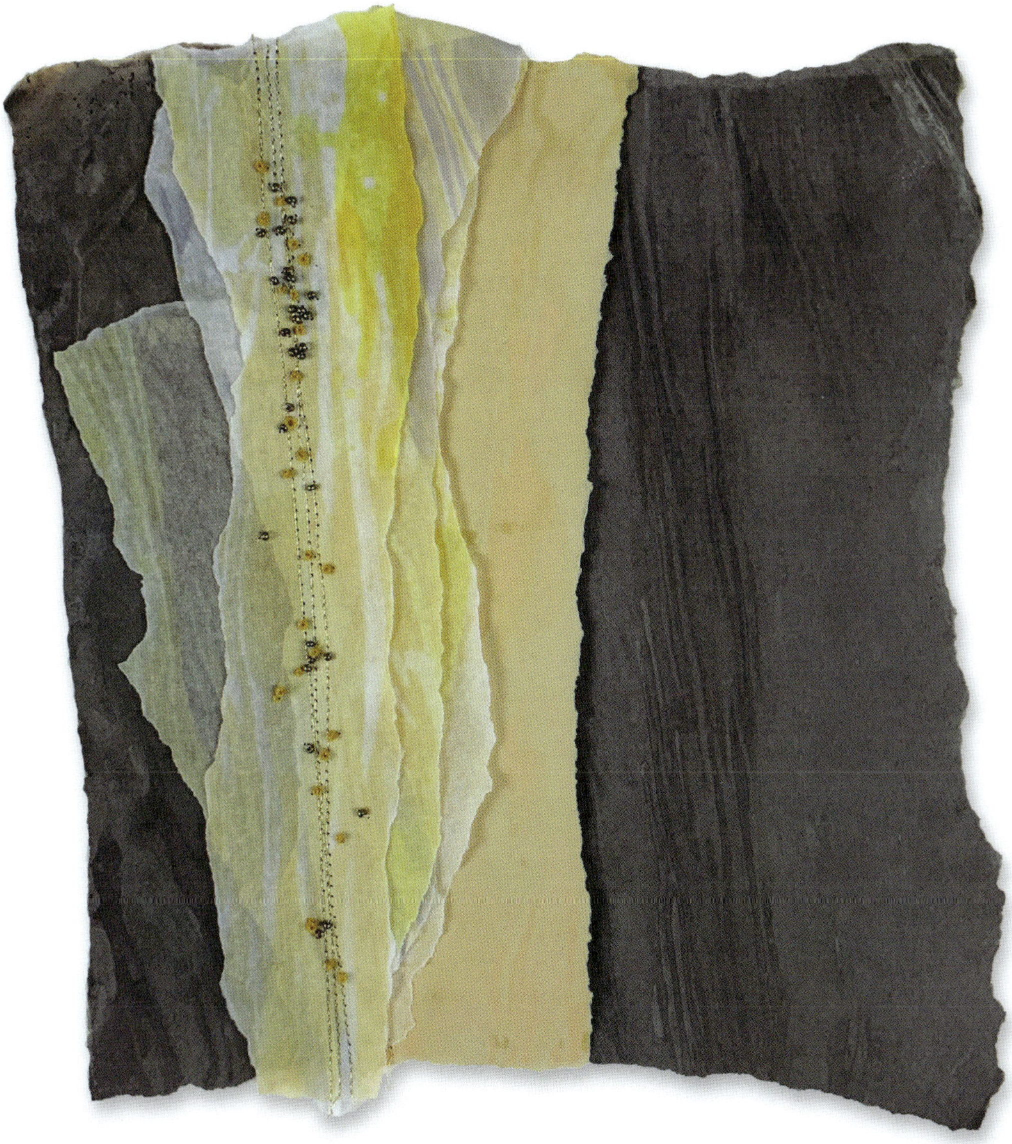

"Summer on the Water" Series.
Botanically-dyed papers and stitch, approx. 9" × 11" (23cm × 28cm)

the daffodils spring up. Ideas of what I would like to do in the studios start to enter my dreams.

I know I will never be the same without Bruce. He colored my life, my hopes, and my dreams. But I know, just as with my artwork, I can't hold onto those moments too tightly or for too long or I will get stuck.

I don't know where my artwork will take me. Will large pieces surface again? Will I work more with paint and less with textiles? Will I start making pinch pots or handmade journals? Will gardens call to me more? I love working in a series. Will that continue? I love the freedom of paint and the simplicity of India ink. Will that continue? I don't know.

With curiosity and play leading the way, though, I need less of the in-between time. I don't need to know where I am going; I can just play.

I step into the unknown, paying attention to my intuition, ready for the next step. And then the next.

TODAY

I am 100 percent cancer free. Yes, 100 percent! It's a remarkable result and means that I am much more likely to stay in remission. It's been several months since my last infusion, and I'm getting stronger every day. My doctors tell me it's likely I had this slow-growing lymphoma for years. I can tell that eventually I will feel stronger than I have in a very long time.

I still grieve the loss of Bruce, of course, but I have joined David Kessler's online grief support training, which has been helpful. My goal when I started was to be able to remember Bruce with more love and less pain. With David Kessler's help, my studios, and time, I know I will get there.

These days I am shocked at the wild and exuberant things that are coming out of me as my journey in the studio continues. I am taking Mark Eanes fabulous online "The Language of Color" class. I'm learning how to control color and think about it analytically as well as intuitively. I lose track of time and find joy in those moments. It's more important now than ever for me to find time in the studio.

I'm making lots of small pieces and turning some of them into cards. I like the thought of them sailing out into the world, hoping they'll land somewhere and bring a moment of joy. It's enough for now.

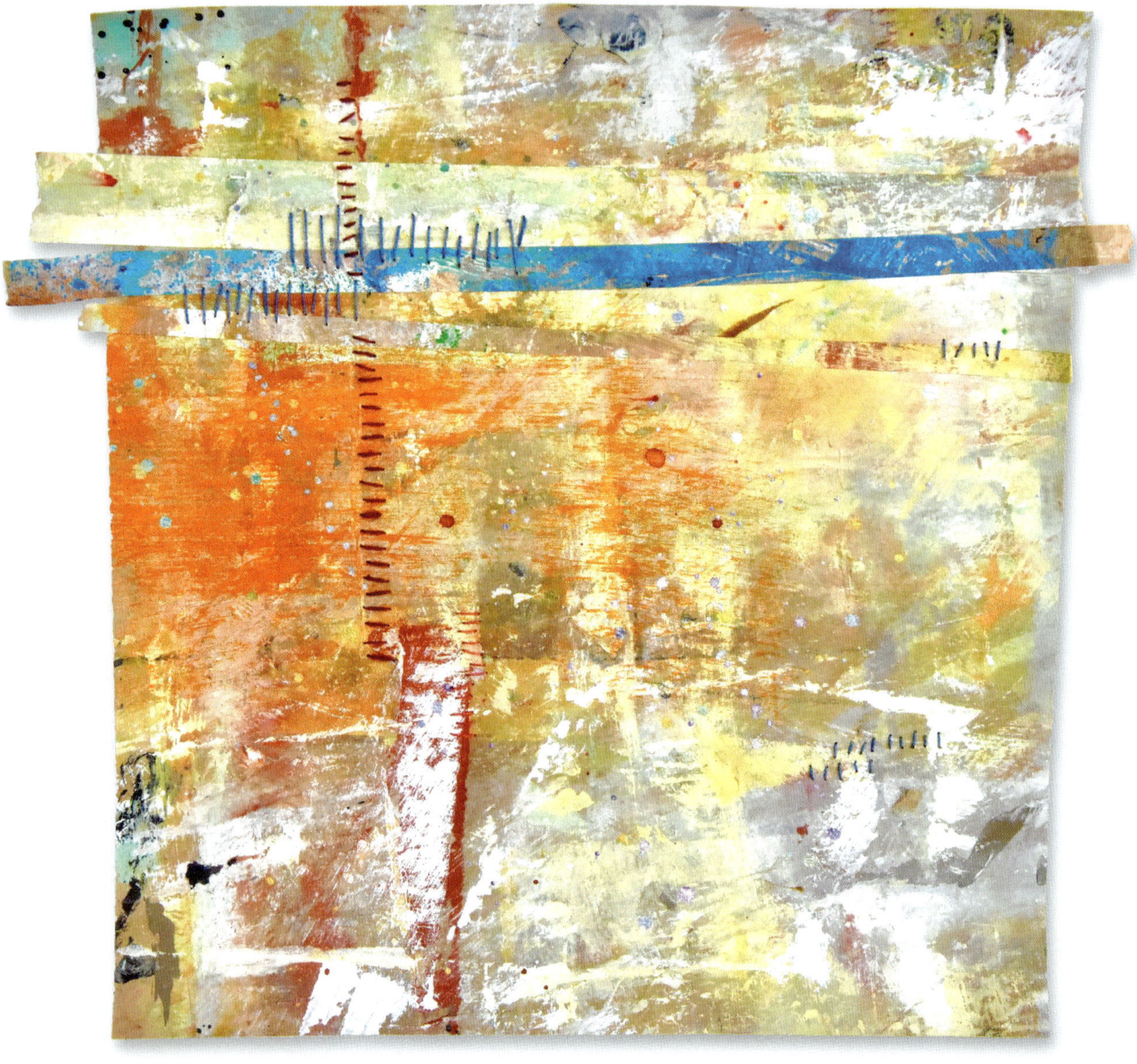

Exuberance
Collage and stitch, 12" x 12" (30cm x 30cm)

AND FINALLY

I've opened those supposedly locked doors that felt closed to me so many years ago.

I've learned to take more risk.

I've learned that when making things, I lose all sense of time and connect with something larger than myself. From that vantage point, the wisdom of the universe touches me. It gives me courage and strength. It heightens my intuition. It reminds me to play and to trust myself. I can accept the messy and difficult parts of life with more grace. I can walk into the unknown with more confidence. I can find joy and love even in times of great sorrow.

It's now so clear to me that making art and gardens is a part of me that desperately wanted to come out into the light. I no longer question why. I am just grateful that I listened.

Our long walk through life gives us so many opportunities to open those locked doors and find more corners of ourselves. I am sure there are more doors to open. I wonder what they will be.

Thank you for walking with me. I send love to you on your walk.

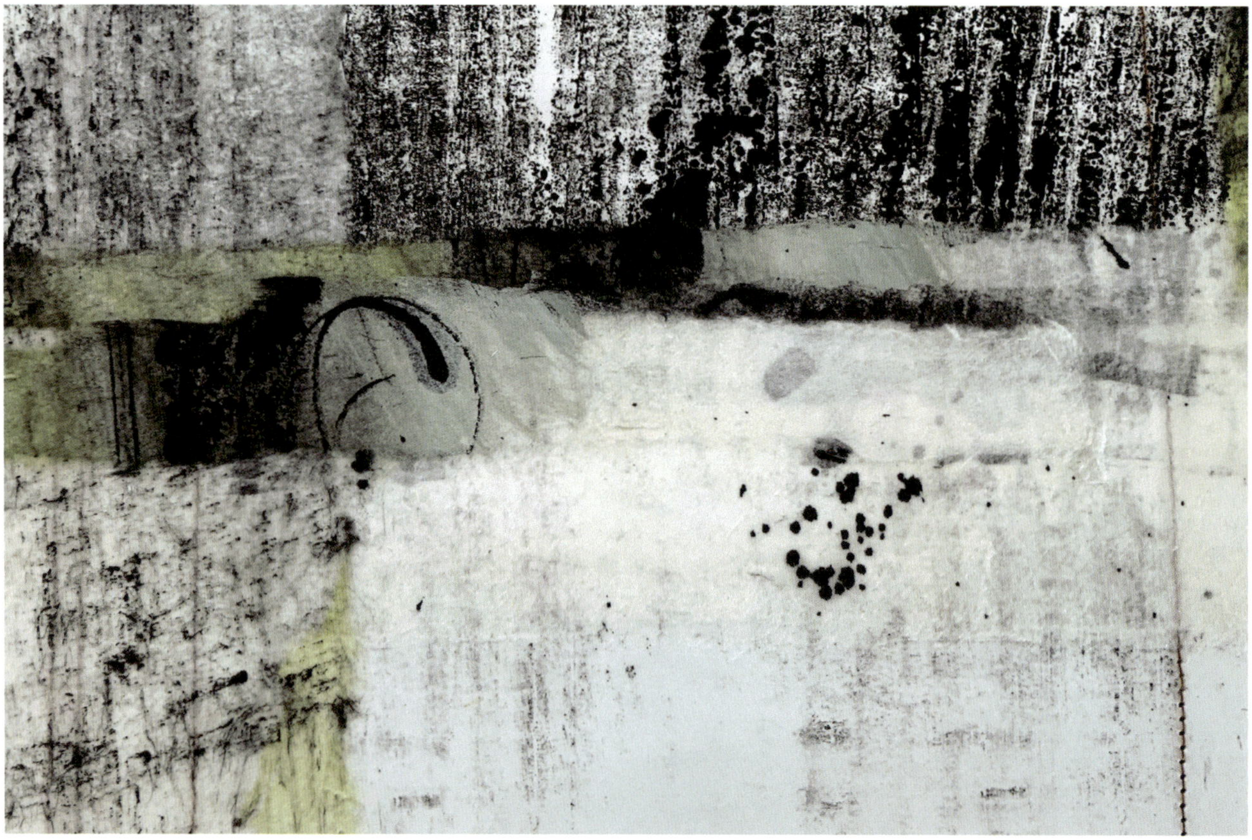

The Unknown
Collage of washi papers and stitch on cardboard, 9" × 5" (23cm × 13cm)

WITH GRATITUDE

A special thank you to Erica Bauermeister, New York Times best-selling author of *The School of Essential Ingredients, Joy for Beginners, The Lost Art of Mixing, The Secret Keeper,* and *House Lessons*. She generously offered insightful comments that helped me to make this a much better book.

Getting good photos for this book was the biggest challenge. Bruce's good friend, John Kirry, who is an excellent photographer, saved the day. Carin Merkle also helped. Heartfelt thanks to both of you.

For my teachers: Vally Possony (for everything); Gail Ferguson (intuition); Jean Houston (Mystery School); Angeles Arrien, Ph.D. (the Institute of Transpersonal Psychology); Dr. Albert C. Barnes and Nicholas King (The Barnes Foundation); Gail Harker (stitch); Nancy Hillis (for bringing me back to paint); Mark Eanes (for the Language of Color); Jane Dunnewold, and India Flint.

For my editors: Jean Munday, Tonia Jenny, and Leslie Heineman.

For the book design: Tonia Jenny

A very special thank you to Robyn Gordon. She shares beautifully curated daily posts on Facebook quoting great thinkers on art, creativity, and life, and then shares the work of artists around the globe. She is herself a talented artist using the medium of wood-carving to create mystical goddesses and totems. She inspires me day after day to search out authors and artists new to me.

For my yoga teachers: Jane Fryer (Iyengar), Lilo Foster (Hatha), Diane Shamsher Bunting (Kundalini).

For my clients, especially Laurie Stewart.

For the authors I love and who have helped me on this journey: Henry Mitchell (my favorite garden writer), Mary Oliver, Dani Shapiro, Natalie Goldberg, Peter Korn, Julia Cameron, Erica Bauermeister, Eckhart Tolle, Elizabeth Gilbert, Kathleen Norris, Anne Truitt, David Whyte, and so many others.

For my mother, Margaret Jane Silvis Wagner, and my father, John Florian Wagner.

For my whole family, especially my sisters: Dr. Kathleen Martin, Susan Hegel, and Mary Morrow.

For my friends who are still traveling with me and those who have moved on.

For being given so many blessings that have made this path easier.

And most especially, thank you, Bruce Alan Bugbee. I am grateful we found each other.

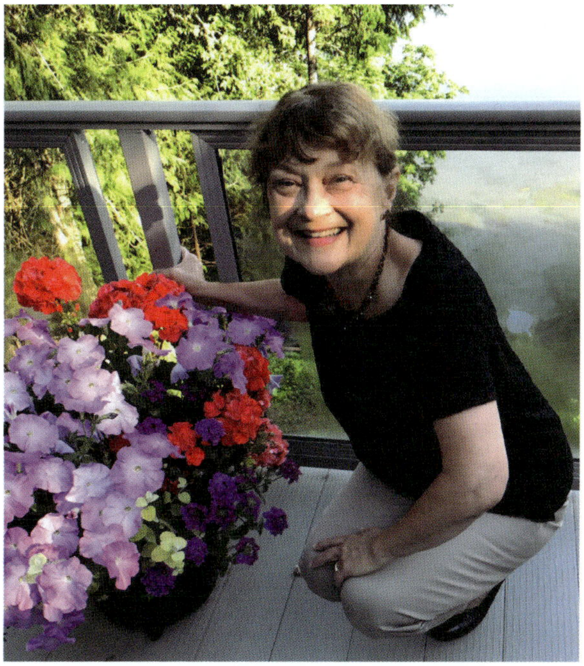

ABOUT ROBERTA WAGNER

This is Roberta Wagner's first book. She wrote for *Clay Times* magazine and has had articles published in a variety of professional magazines. She has studied with Vally Possony, Jean Houston, Gail Ferguson, Nancy Hillis, India Flint, Mark Eanes, and many other artists and potters. She has a degree in international relations with a concentration in economics from Hamline University in Saint Paul, Minnesota, and a master's degree from the Institute of Transpersonal Psychology. She also completed the two-year art education program at The Barnes Foundation in Philadelphia, Pennsylvania. Roberta has shown her artwork in various galleries in Washington, D.C., Virginia, and Washington state, and completed an eight-foot diameter fountain for the Lewis Ginter Botanical Garden in Richmond, Virginia.

Please visit www.robertawagner.com and connect with her on Instagram.

Printed in the United States of America

First Printing, 2021

ISBN-13: 978-1-7354105-0-0 (Paperback edition)

Editors: Leslie J. Heineman, Tonia Jenny

Designer: Tonia Jenny www.toniajenny.com

Published by Roberta Wagner

www.robertawagner.com

Printed in Great Britain
by Amazon

69387037R00093